THE
VIRTUAL
HELP DESK
Strategic Management Center

The
VIRTUAL
HELP DESK

Strategic
Management
Center

ANDREW H. THOMAS
with ROBERT M. STEELE

A SOLOMON PRESS BOOK

International Thomson Computer Press

I(T)P™ A Division of International Thomson Publishing Inc.
New York • Albany • Bonn • Boston • Detroit • London • Madrid • Melbourne
Mexico City • Paris • San Francisco • Singapore • Tokyo • Toronto

Contents

List of Tables

List of Figures

List of Photographs

Preface

*T*HE PURPOSE OF THIS BOOK IS TO SHARE IDEAS, knowledge and expertise that the authors have gleaned over many years as consultants in the help desk domain. The book is about computer help desks, but this fact does not make it inappropriate for other types of help desks. The audience for this book is anyone who is providing help desks, formally or informally, or anyone who is thinking about providing them, or anyone who is simply interested in the subject. The information and case studies cited in this book are from diverse situations that represent large and small, established and start-up support centers.

The book has six sections. The first section provides a primer on the service industry as a business and examines some critical success factors. It also explains the general topic of computer service and its evolution from a product support function into a viable and profitable business enterprise. The second section familiarizes the reader with the definition of help desks, their purpose, why they are becoming more important in today's mercurial economy, and their values and benefits. Section 3 addresses a new concept—the *management center*. We believe the help desk of today will soon emerge into this type of arrangement. Section 4 looks at evaluating and implementing help desk software—daunting tasks for the uninitiated. Section 5 presents three actual case studies involving help desks, and the manner in which international industry leaders have implemented them to substantially improve their market position. Section 6 comprises four appendices.

Our book offers two important benefits to the reader: The first is sharing actual in-house, on-site experience by way of real-life examples. Circumstances, environments, and goals are numerous and diverse for most help desk owners, but it is always inviting to explore how someone else approaches the same problem, even if it occurs in a completely different business. There is certainly no such thing as a stereotypical model; however, some of the methods and ideas offered may provide the basis for an improvement in the readers' concepts about support centers. The second benefit is the inspiration of new thinking about help desks. An example of this is the model algorithm for capturing productivity. The formula and assumptions may not be relevant to everyone, everywhere, but the idea of a finite way to measure the value-added is important to consider.

Any book on computers usually has a threshold of complexity—a point (or points) when the English language seems to turn into an impossible foreign tongue. Your authors have tried hard to be empathetic and to stay away from acronyms and discussions of hyper-complexity. Some of the material in this book may seem elementary, for which apologies are offered. These few elementary descriptions may, however, add to the unversed reader's help desk knowledge.

You are reading this book because *you need help*—help in understanding more about support hot lines so that you can develop one in your own organization or improve the operation of one that is already in service. Maybe you simply need a better understanding of hotlines.

Man's (male nouns hereinafter refer to men *and* women) nature is to seek help throughout his life, in every pursuit and situation. Help and helping are essential and integral parts of our lives, taking on multiple dimensions. If we weren't helped by our parents from birth and during our formative years, we would not be here today. If teachers had not helped us in school, we would be very different from what we are. Our friends have helped us; and so it goes—we *all* depend on help.

This book is about that important job of providing assistance, primarily with computer systems, including hardware and software. Most of the readers of this book are providers of technical services, or they have the capacity and interest to do so. The concepts presented here are also applicable to providing assistance in almost any environment in which user help is needed. Two distinctly different groups of people will find this book useful: those who provide computers and associated applications to users, and those responsible for supporting internal and/ or external customers in a variety of computing endeavors. *Computers* refers to the machines or hardware that do the computing as well as the software or programs that instruct the hardware in what to do. Users need both.

Bob Steele is an unusually talented person whose background in help desks was critical in developing this book. Bob is the "inventor" of the management center concept.

This is my second book produced by The Solomon Press. Sidney and Raymond Solomon, partners in The Solomon Press, were indispensable, and their help and patience are much appreciated.

John Hutchinson, a colleague for over twenty years, knows the subject, and we thank him for his insightful review of the original manuscript.

Kathy Robbins a help desk expert helped in reviewing and Judy Meyers did an outstanding job of copy editing.

Finally, Nat and Jake offered their grateful support when things got sticky.

—*Andrew H. Thomas*
September 1995

Prologue

ECHNOLOGY HAS BECOME PART OF OUR SOCIETY, and we have traded the Industrial Revolution for the Knowledge Revolution. Personal computers, decision tools, groupware, business and personal networks, and the ever present "information highway" are all being introduced to us at a staggering pace. Technology has moved so fast that all of us are having a difficult time understanding what it has done to us in our personal and professional lives. To really understand the direction in which technology is taking us, and to thereby understand our own relative position in the scheme of things, we really need to understand the historical perspective of technology.

In the beginning was the word . . . 8 bits for the most part. Because technology was in its infancy, "big" was a natural starting point. Brainiac, the first working computer with all its vacuum tubes, led to refinements resulting in solid-state gates and so on, from the proprietary mainframes to the mid-range and mini-range systems we see today. What was occurring then? The high tech industry was mainly focused on getting computers and operating systems functioning as hosts for applications that actually did something. High tech vendors were developing a raw, empty brain that could be filled with information and knowledge, and each company had its own vision of how this brain should be designed. What is happening now? Users have settled on the design (or designs) of the brain and have turned their focus to filling those brains with something useful.

High tech companies whose focus has traditionally been to design, build, sell, and maintain faster, cheaper boxes will either change their core business or fail. The competition in building and selling "brains" is so high that the required margins for supporting the typically large infrastructures of the high tech companies are no longer attainable. Anyone can now build a "brain," but not everyone can educate it. In our immediate futures we will see that some of the most prestigious companies in our industry change, merged into other companies, or simply fade into a technologically curious history. Big is no longer beautiful nor necessarily functional. We believe that the large corporate structure like the obsolescence of the Brainiac, will be replaced with smaller, faster, cheaper, distributed, shared organizations.

The main characteristics of our technological brain have been stabilized, for the moment. Of course, refinements will be made to make it faster, cheaper, etc., but there will be a hiatus in this development during which the user will be focused on the content of this brain. Applications and their use, decision tools, groupware and the resulting global dialogue: In the beginning was the word, but this word is now thirty-two or sixty-four bits. It is now the seventh day and our turn in the garden. Take a byte. . . .

The Technology Garden and You

If you are reading this, you are probably a help desk professional, or at least we hope so. Help desk is our profession, and our intent in this book is to promote both you and ourselves in an industry that has for years relegated us to a secondary role in Information Technology (IT) management. What does all the new technology and the coming knowledge era mean to you? Lots, if you can cope and if you can keep up with technology; if you can fight all odds and really focus on users; if you can acknowledge some very basic facts about support; if you are serious about being a true help desk professional.

Here are nine fundamentals of the help desk:

1. Don't ignore the problem.

As help desk professionals, our role was generally subordinate to a service or IT management function. Our superiors were specialists in the "management sciences," which all too often thought BIG (much like Brainiac). Rarely did they listen to the needs of the help desk, thereby, ignoring users. The users will now get their revenge. The final decision for our technological "brain" is now, in fact, the users themselves; even though they are distributed in nature, their power is all that much more enhanced by the enabling of their distributed knowledge.

2. Always stay close to the user.

Technology is at a point today where it has shifted its focus from cranial design to filling the gray matter it created. The war of "proprietaries" is over, and the brain of this generation, at least, comes from people like Bill Gates. Users have begun, on their own, to ignore big and do what they knew was needed all along. They have simply accepted one of many brains and started to fill the gray void themselves with no real care for proprietors. The user could care less which is better—better in our industry has never had anything to do with acceptance. No one will argue that IBM did not build a better brain than MicroSoft—it has no relevance to users at all.

3. Think "Off the shelf."

Since we have established the acceptance of a global brain, we need to focus on content rather than architecture. If the needs of your business are not already developed somewhere, you are probably either lying to yourself, have not found them yet, or are in the less than 1 percent of IT organizations that have specific, unique requirements for their specific industry.

4. Outsource.

If you have unique requirements, have someone else build the application. You are not in the application development business. You are a help desk professional. Many companies today are developing their own help desk applications on the belief that they have their own specific and unique requirements. Apologies to our readers who are doing this, but in all likelihood you are wasting time and money. In the combined years these authors have been in the business, there are *very* few such companies.

There are hundreds of help desk packages on the market. Trust us—one of them meets your needs. Someone, somewhere may prove us wrong, but if they are trying to "go it alone," they are making a mistake. Buying a package or outsourcing the development of the truly "unique" package at least enables you, the help desk professional, to sue someone for failure. Not so with internal resources. We have simply seen too many failures on this path (which is like trying to remove your own appendix).

5. Be willing to be downsized.

The true help desk professional should be willing to streamline his business to the point where he is no longer needed. Downsizing will be a way of life for all of us in the long term; as professionals we should have a personal philosophy that puts us in harm's way. This sounds rather extreme, but consider the fact that in the vast majority of cases where help desk professionals have accepted and promoted this philosophy, they have either been promoted within or recognized in the industry for their abilities and hired externally to propagate their success. Don't view downsizing as a threat—see it as an opportunity.

6. Commit to reading.

There is no way to remain a help desk professional without a strict reading regimen. Remaining current with technology and trends and finding a better way to integrate tools or providing better service is your job. The number of periodicals available to you is unending, and the vast majority of them are free. Develop a reading list and set aside a fixed amount of time daily for this discipline. Your reading should include industry news from both the IT industry and your own company's industry. It should include reading material specific to the help desk and publications by associations that specialize in the help desk function.

7. Join an association.

There are a number of associations that specialize in help desks and management tools. Pick one, join one, and network with other members in your same situation. They have already made the mistakes you want to avoid.

8. Think management center.

The help desk is growing obsolete and is rapidly being replaced with the concept of a management center. Begin to focus on the evolution of our industry and understand that the evolution of the help desk is moving with technology. Every day, more management functions are becoming embedded in the source code of myriad applications. Go with the flow. Most importantly, understand the flow.

Your position in the help desk profession puts you in the dead center of this evolution. Senior management in companies will survive only if their orientation becomes more technical. Help desk professionals will need to orient themselves more toward business. The corporate manager of the future is a composite or hybrid of the senior and middle managers of the Industrial Revolution. These hybrids will be technocrats. CEOs as we all know and love them will be replaced by technologists who will relinquish operational command and direct a distributed technology strategy and plan.

Business planning and operational planning in most corporations is a career for many. They will be gone and replaced with applications if they have not already been replaced. Applications such as MicroSoft Assistant and IBM/Lotus Notes will move the planning function to a template and groupware driven process, which is more focused on strategy, implementation, and management than it is on politics, format, and structure of a document. As a help desk professional you will be at the heart of this process. Have it go through you, not over you.

9. Think integration.

The management center of the future is not here yet. A help desk system that fully integrates all the necessary management functions for a true management center—the Holy Grail for us help desk professionals—does not exist today. Each and every function can be addressed with some application on the shelf, but no integrator, vendor, or developer has really focused on pulling these applications together. You will either need to do it yourself or force your vendors to do it for you, the latter being the preferred approach. We are not talking about rocket science here. We are talking about integrating existing products and tools and applying them to the management sciences. To do this, you must look beyond the call desk. Do this, and you will be the hybrid manager who evolves with technology.

Service as a Business Enterprise

Chapter

1

The Changing Service Industry

All machinery is on an irresistible march to the junk heap and its progress, while it may be delayed, cannot be prevented by repairs.
—Hatfield

THIS RATHER STARK ASSESSMENT OF THE THINGS we build for the betterment of humanity points to the importance of our profession. No matter how well manufacturers make things, products are certain to require some form of service and support in their product life cycle. Service is the art of making good on someone else's mistake.

All too often we get wrapped up in the state of technology and products. The focus for us as service managers and help desk professionals should not be the product. Our focus must be on the user and the business he is trying to conduct. Technology has become part of our society, with personal computers and desktop computers producing an ever expanding array of products in virtually every market sector. Computer systems are usually maintained by the vendors, with third-party service organizations capturing an increasing market share of services in recent years. Both have trouble coping with the sheer volume and variety of computer-based devices that must be maintained. One thing is certain: the User often determines the selection of a vendor according to his perception of the availability and quality of service it offers.

In the past, users have had little to say about the products they use, with a corporate function determining product selection. With the trend to distributed processing, the selection of products is getting closer to the user, with a corporate function establishing standards rather than specific vendors or products. In the future, users will base their selection of products on their applicability to the business and the support capabilities of the vendor.

Satisfaction with the availability and quality of service is a major factor in a consumer's decision to purchase computer equipment. According to a survey by Prognostics, 45 percent of the reasons cited for rejection of a particular product are service related. No potential customer purchases a system without being assured that downtime will be minimal. The manufacturer must be able to guarantee dependable, effective, and speedy maintenance. It should be noted that our definition of *customer* in this context is evolving from the customer as a central purchasing function to a customer as an empowered user working in a distributed corporate world.

Service and support, according to William Davidow and Bro Uttal in their book, *Total Customer Service*, is the next frontier of competition. Earlier concepts of computer service centered around the provision of hardware maintenance through a field engineering force. Typically, manufacturers' field offices were split into sales and support with the sales organization generating gross margin on products shipped, and the support organization usually being a cost center to deal with installation and upkeep of those products. Today, hardware maintenance is a declining element of the revenues of these service organizations, and the concept of support has changed dramatically from those days. In order to meet the challenges of the remainder of the '90s, service providers are changing, and will continue to change, their business processes. Many of today's viable hardware manufacturers have successfully marketed their technology with little or no service organization. They outsource their service needs. By doing so, they have not only created a virtual service organization but they have also built sales channels and services that are more regionally focused.

Another approach in services is the multi-vendor customer service (MCS) organization. This means that a particular manufacturer will now service most anything his customer wants serviced (including competitors' equipment) whereas a few years ago touching anyone else's equipment was not done. The MCS provides hardware maintenance for a range of different manufacturers' hardware, and is in the service business to make a profit. It incorporates software services in its portfolio. Its selling proposition is to provide a single point of contact for any hardware or software problem. Because MCS' focused on service management, they are generally more efficient than the manufacturers at providing that service. Thus they can offer "one stop shopping" at a price lower than the aggregate of the various different manufacturers. The change from the finger-pointing, individualized service to a single point of contact for support has been very helpful for customers but is creating some problems with MCS firms. More parts, more training and more systems are not easy to manage. Competitive pricing pressures also exist and this has taken its toll amongst some service firms and third-party maintainers. Acquisitions have been made on the grounds that service organizations gain a great deal from economies of scale. Certainly it seems that larger organizations benefit from the flexibility that goes with a large service engineering force, for example, but they are also more difficult to manage.

Other events having an impact on traditional maintenance service include the advent of the desktop computer and lower-cost software packages, local area networking (LAN), E-mail, and groupware, provide opportunities for growth. Although these products are inexpensive to purchase, the installation and support of the integrated package is often tricky, requiring service skills that are very valuable. These requirements by end users have given service firms new opportunities, including outsourcing the entire information systems effort, and service too.

Typically today, services may include installing large quantities of desk top computers configured to customized specifications, and wired into the company LAN software and groupware need to be installed. Corollary services might include training the customer end users, setting up a help desk, communications linkages and perhaps project management. The exraordinary demand for these types of services today is creating a real focus on developing the services as a separate business enterprise.

Users are less frequently buying service for a list of unbundled products, item by item, with various contract start dates, but by other parameters such as site, usage of the hardware/ services, (like a utility—gas or electricity) or applications. Some service customers are coming to the conclusion that they no longer want to own products but to pay for services (with vendor-provided current technology) at a fixed periodic price.

While many of the larger product vendors have tried to deliver these types of services, the greatest problems they encounter are internal. The first barrier is financial: long-term risk and the return on investment. Since this type of service is itself very complex, selling to internal control organizations is extremely difficult. Another barrier is the internal conflicts resulting from departmental politics. Since most of these contracts are high dollar and high visibility, infighting for control of the contract commences from day one. Additionally, sales representatives are quick to recognize that this type of contract squeezes them out of the picture. Most high tech vendors continue to set sales metrics that mandate product sales; in this case as well as in outsourcing deals, the customer representative loses the customer.

It can be seen from these changes that hardware maintenance has given way, in the service organizations we are dealing with, to what is now termed "integrated, multi-vendor services." *Integrated*, because delivery of a range of services requires interaction between these services. *Multi-vendor* because the products supplied and serviced are produced by a range of different manufacturers. This range of responsibilities often means that the prime service provider may have to use the expertise of other, external, organizations to deliver some of its products.

The desire to build large service organizations, along with the demolition of trade barriers, has encouraged another important development in the service market—the global service company. For example, benefits can be obtained from both internationally held logistics operations and costly specialist support groups that make their expertise available throughout several countries (versus one costly group in each country). This type of organization not only has the usual management complexities associated with running a large service business but it also has to deal with geographic, cultural, and economic boundaries. Without good information systems, it is likely that the management problems of running international service companies would outweigh the gains from the economies of scale. For the immediate future, the MCS that is quickest to provide seamless services across national, cultural, and divisional borders will be the big winner in the service and support business. Nevertheless, issues such as international warranty, warranty period and cost, pricing, etc.—issues that have caused nightmares for service and help desk managers since the beginning—will have to be addressed. The greatest barrier to solving these issues is usually an internal problem revolving around metrics and justification of infrastructure. The metrics issue in most large multinationals continues to haunt the large vendors. Over the years, the stress on box-driven sales created a set of metrics that were established to protect sales representatives from each other. Sales credit and the resulting commissions created an environment that was designed to reduce squabbling and protect individual turfs. This practice continues today, with the customer being less of a concern than where they happen to be doing business.

Consider a large multinational that would like to buy at the enterprise level for product distribution worldwide. The typical exercise in this case is to communicate separately with each country to establish specific pricing and terms. Even within the subsidiaries of the large vendors, there remains no consensus or standards too quickly and easily produce a quote for a customer. In previous years, a large contingent of staff were established to break through these problems by specializing in communicating with various countries to get the necessary information. Rather than being a solution for a historical problem, they have become today's problem by fighting any efforts to systematize and computerize the process. They fight and hinder the process, for the consequences for them is obsolescence. Due to these difficulties, "in-country" staff were put in place. Efforts to make each

Table 1-1 The changing nature of services

Service Aspect	1970s	1980s	1990s	2000s
Service Business	Cost Center	Profit Center	Business Unit	Division
Service Pricing	What The Market Will Bear	TPMs Drive Prices Down	Fair Value	Custom and Cost Plus
Help Desks	De Facto–Laissez Faire	Dispatching and Call Handling	Entitlement—Fewer On-Site Calls	Distributed—Added Management Functions
Service Technology	High Training Costs—Specialists— Hard Copy Documentation	Improved Diagnostics— Self Help— Parts Depots	Interactive— Artificial Intelligence—On-site Call Avoidance	Increased level of knowledge base tools, and automated functions such as network management
Service Attitude	Caveat Emptor—Service CashCow	The Rise In Service Quality	Service As A Competitive Advantage	More focus on business issues and less on technical expertise
Hardware & Software	Different Service Offerings and Organizations	Merger of Hardware and Software Service	Same Service Arm Does Both Hardware and Software Service	Full Suite services such as ITUtilities
Service Delivery	Specialists	Swap Out Faulty Part	Generalists	Home based Knowledge Workers, follow the sun

subsidiary conform to standards, thereby easing the systematization and computerization of various sales and service processes, are blocked, even sabotaged, for the same self-obsolescence problems. The large multinational vendors will cite legal, cultural, import/export law, and subsidiary laws to explain why they have not provided multinational, multi-year sales and service contracts. The bottom line, however, comes to a bloated infrastructure defending itself against obsolescence.

Key Changes in Management Style and Their Impact on IT

Service providers must respond to changes in the service market and consequently are making further demands on their

IT systems providers. The profound nature of the changes in service supply have led to a need for process reengineering in our customer organizations. The processes that supported a field service force of maintenance engineers are not applicable to the integrated multi-vendor services supplied today. Many organizations have evolved their current processes as market conditions have changed, but few have taken advantage of IT to reinvent existing processes to optimize their business. Requirements of the service industry and experiences of companies who have undertaken process reengineering reveal a number of changes in organization structure and management style.

The Japanese renaissance of quality started a trend toward more worker care and initiative, which had been the responsibility of the quality control department of a quality specialist(s). This endeavor, often referred to as TQM (Total Quality Management), is a process whereby every worker makes incremental improvements in the manufacturing or production process to enhance product demand and market share. Hammer & Champy's Business Process Re-engineering (BPR) also focuses on process, but this particular strategy is employed to shorten or simplify procedures which take inordinate amounts of time and cost to perform. The individual employee must have the power to make unilateral decisions to achieve results in order for either TQM or BPR strategy to work, and he needs information in order to enable him to make the *right* decision. Timely and correct information must be readily accessible from company systems and data bases to facilitate these decisions. This data must be controlled by the system to accommodate both the employee, in his work and the company, in terms of security.

Individual employees are also trending towards more generalizations of the work chores they perform in lieu of the division of labor principle which began with industrial revolution. This trend has accelerated via the desktop revolution; and systems improvements can provide specialist knowledge which removes the need for experts to support individual aspects of carrying out a process. For example, an obligation management system containing rules of billing obviates the need for a billing specialist. Several "specialist" functions have been eliminated by intelligent systems which produce critical information to a single generalist who now has complete control over a whole business process.

To meet the needs of the generalist worker, systems must provide easy access to information. This information is usually in separate places as multiple elements of the system. If all these elements were under the aegis of a single software vendor, a fully integrated "package" could be expected. As this is not the case, it is necessary to link together systems from different vendors.

Chapter

2

The Business of Support Services

RECENT RESEARCH BY INTERNATIONAL DATA CORPORA-
TION (IDC)* reveals that the overall market for system support
services will continue to grow slightly. A somewhat more opti-
mistic forecast is documented for worldwide service revenues
than for those generated in the United States. With traditional
break/fix services no longer generating sufficient profits, service
providers have been developing other service offerings that will
both meet customer needs and furnish service providers with
more sizable profit margins.

The IDC report indicates that the system support services
market will experience a compound annual growth rate (CAGR)
of 1.3 percent in the United States from 1994 through 1999,
with a total market size of $15 billion. Worldwide, the CAGR
comes to 11.4 percent, with revenues totaling $62 billion by

---

*Source: International Data Corporation, 1994. Caution is recommended in the use of
available studies. While we cannot ignore the wealth of information provided by available studies, we should also not ignore our own common sense and judgment in using
them. Selection of available studies is usually based on a geographic market, but many
service management and help desk professionals can be impacted by trends in other
geographies. This impact cannot be ignored, especially as the industry heads toward
international, multi-year warranties and service contracts.

1999. IDC believes that the slightly better forecast for worldwide revenues is also a result of the fact that the rest of the world is behind in installing newer technologies such as optical drives or the latest printers, which have already been a part of the IT picture in the United States for a number of years.

The biggest segment of this market continues to be parts support, with $5.7 billion spent in the United States in 1994. In this same year, customers spent $4.7 billion for on-site hardware troubleshooting services. However, on-site hardware trouble-shooting shows a 7.5 percent CAGR in spending through 1997, while the parts support shows a 1.5 percent CAGR.

Although overall the system support services market will re-main flat, the outlook is better when the market is segmented by specific types of services. Solid growth is forecast for online knowledge-based services (67.7 percent five-year CAGR); asset management services (53.9 percent); bulletin board services (44.7 percent); predictive maintenance services (17 percent); and systems management services (14 percent).

With break/fix no longer as profitable a business as it used to be, service providers need to refine their offerings in areas such as asset management and preventive maintenance. The sup-port services market is defined as procurement of outside ser-vices to install, manage, and maintain IT products and systems.

Despite the dramatic changes in the service industry, the service function has come a long way. Once considered by read-ers a necessary evil that was often a serious drain on cash flow, service has become critically important today as a provider of customer satisfaction and as a dependable source of revenue that can be extremely profitable. Companies of all sizes, in nearly every industry in our economy, have found they can now rely on the service function to make a significant contribution to the bottom line; service has become a money-making business on its own. Whether through third-party maintenance organizations or the manufacturers' own service groups, purchasers of equip-ment are more than willing to spend money to keep their sys-tems running, to upgrade or update their systems, or to make modifications that increase productivity or eliminate bugs. How much revenue can field service account for? Consider three points:

1. Companies often spend more on maintaining a system during its lifetime than they do on buying it.

2. Most manufacturers reap more than half their total profits from service. In some cases, all of the profits were gleaned from the service organizations.

3. Multi-vendor customer service is currently a multi-billion-dollar industry and growing.

Looked at from any of these three ways, there is a significant opportunity for companies to profit from services. The financial state of high-tech companies provides clear evidence of the importance of service. It seems that mostly high-tech information systems firms address service in their annual reports, narratively and financially.

If IBM's service business were to stand alone as a separate company, that hypothetical company would be on the Fortune 100 list. Their service business is almost as big as the *entire* business of Digital™ or Unisys™, and is slightly larger than such well-known companies as Caterpillar™ and Raytheon™.

Gross margins of service businesses are perhaps even more impressive than the service revenue picture. In most cases, service gross margins exceed those of the *total* corporate gross margins. Stockholders should be very thankful for service, as earnings per share are often highly influenced by the service business.

With the break/fix type of service waning because of more reliable equipment, shorter product life cycles, and smarter customers, service cash cows that were prevalent in the 1970s, are no longer as profitable. Several companies have addressed this issue of replacing revenues by adding new, chargeable, functions. Table 2-1 shows a sample of some of the new activities that are falling under the services umbrella.

By the end of the '90s, many of the services mentioned will have become obsolete themselves. Network management functions will become more automated, and, indeed, the network architectures themselves will have changed as the proprietary networks of today give way to utilities provided by the survivors of the telecommunications and cable company wars.

Table 2-1 New service activities are helping to replace the cash cow break/fix services

Operations Support Services
Services Management Support
Services Administrative Support
Logistics Support Services
Strategic Service Consulting
Facilities Management Services

Installation & Start-up Services

Training Packages and Plans

Product Support Services
Basic System Support
Software Support Service
Node Service
Layered Product Support
Multi-vendor Software Services
Mission-critical Support Service
Software System Management
   Service
Software Update Installation Service
Media and Documentation Distribu-
   tion Service
Documentation Update Service

Network Consulting Services
Requirements Analysis
Design Analysis
Application Design Service
Protocol Design Service
Physical Design Service

Network Management Services

Local Area Interconnect Support
Wide Area Interconnect Support
NETsupport Shared LAN Service
NETsupport Shared TCP/IP Service
NETsupport Advisory Support
Network Onsite Consulting
Open Systems Distributed Computing
   Services

Desktop Services
Staging Service
User System Support
Total System Support
Laptop Mail-in Service
Connectivity Service
Network Documentation Service
Software Update Installation
System Performance Tuning

Business Protection Services
Asset Management
Contingency Planning Assistance
Disaster Recovery Services
Restart Service
Moving Service
Data Protection Service
Environmental Products
Site Planning, Design, and Implemen-
   tation

Provision of services "on demand" via satellite, cable, or existing municipal infrastructures such as electric service will push the office closer to the home environment: location will no longer be critical for availability of optimum capacity, speed, and bandwidth. Users will pay for their workstation and services in one monthly billing that will include hardware and software usage. In this same time period, we may even see the demise of the workstation itself as new HDTV television designs hit the street with built-in computing functions and only a separate keyboard to distinguish it from a normal TV. Maybe Commodore did have it right years ago? We have visions of the kids fighting over which channel they want, Channel 4 MSC or Channel 5 ACN (MSC being the MicroSoft™ Channel; APM, the Apple™ Computer Network). Bets are that channel 4's ratings will be higher!

Chapter

3

New Templates for Service Delivery

*T*O UNDERSTAND THE NEWER MODES OF DELIVERING computer service, we must follow how it was done in the beginning.
From the 1950s through the early to mid 1970s, field service
was delivered by a field service representative, on-site, following
a call to the service department of the product manufacturer. In
fact, at its very basic level, this was one of the first forms of
outsourcing in our industry.

Call handling was performed manually, by dispatchers, and
service orders were passed through a number of hands before
the calls were closed—if they ever were closed. Parts were or-
dered against lead times that sometimes were as long as six to
seven months and were managed using a simple Rolodex and
index card system. Huge amounts of inventory were scrapped
because of newer revisions of the same part. When it came time
to take an inventory accounting, clever district managers would
ship the parts back to the logistics center so they would not be
charged for the inventory. Service firms treated parts in the air
or en route at zero value right about budget time. Response
times were usually next day for critical accounts—that is, the
ones who did not have service engineers working from on-site

offices. A service engineer who was dedicated to a particular site frequently became an employee of the customer. The charge for a dedicated on-site service person was typically one-hundred thousand dollars per annum back in the early 1970s. Training for large systems usually took about ten months. This was very expensive, in terms of both the utilization of engineers and the customers' needs. The service engineer in those days had to be very strong, or they needed a sizable dolly to carry all the documentation needed to diagnose and solve the problem.

More often than not a second site visit was required to deliver and install the spare part that was needed. Many firms employed a roving parts truck in larger cities in an effort to speed up the process (the "Man in the Van" concept). Service engineers would often work all night in order to give the customer a working system by the next shift. There were also hazards involved. One New York service engineer parked his car outside the entrance of a large insurance company in mid-Manhattan. When he returned the car was gone. Because the car was so critical to his service delivery, he bought another one and put the cost through on his weekly expense report!

As the installed base of computer companies grew, so did the need for more service managers. Many were simply service engineers who were smart and showed good management skills. Few were college graduates, as most were hired right out of two-year technical or electronics schools, or they were people separating from an electronics background in the military. Of the latter, there was an abundance due to an active draft system and global hostilities. Career growth was promising and swift.

The rapid growth of computer service organizations also led to sluggish and overstaffed service divisions, even today. One of the largest computer companies even now has over 100 people who do nothing but price services for the company's products. This is done by estimating what the service will cost and adding a margin, or, most often, by establishing a price that is competitive to other similar products on the market. The unusual point here is that the company's management reports are so limited that the originator of the service price can never tell what the exact margins are for the products he has priced. Another irony is the fact that in spite of the science and head count applied to pricing of services, the exercise will very often be wasted. In the end, senior management, sales, or marketing types will ignore the recommended pricing and establish an arbitrary price that was developed through no other science but market position.

In their heyday, service groups were often overstaffed with clever service engineers and managers who needed "job enrichment" to stay stimulated. One service organization even employed psychologists to cater to the service organization's prima donnas, among others. They proved, through formal surveys and testing, that service people were psychologically different from salespersons. Salespeople love money; service people love problems they can solve.

The golden years of service were soon to mature and yield to tremendous cost-consciousness and the financial pressures of a business enterprise rather than those of a sales support function. A large impetus for this movement was the advent and continuation of third-party maintenance. The third-party maintenance phenomenon brought irrationally high service prices to more competitive levels.

How will the successful cyber-service businesses deliver services in the future? Firstly, customers demand more flexibility from their service providers. This means that service must be available not, for example, on a shift basis, but on a demand basis. During most of the year, a retail operation can take a routine service contract. But during the hectic holiday periods, it must be certain to have enhanced coverage to respond to the seasonal buying patterns of its customers. As mentioned earlier, break/fix services are diminishing, and more consultive type services will take the form of projects and professional services. This means that contract structures will have to change to accommodate the newer services.

The tools used by service businesses will allow more knowledge to be dispersed more often and in less time and for less cost than earlier. Instead of training several service representatives for many months, knowledge can be banked at either a central headquarters or regionally, and dispensed, via internet or other networks, to the workforce, to more unskilled or entry-level individuals. The data files and libraries at a central location contain a wealth of information that by wire, wireless, or satellite, can be conveyed to practically any other location in the world. The service representative can use a combination of laptop computer, telephone, facsimile, beeper, or radio to receive information to fix or attend to the problem. This information may take the form of written text, schematic diagrams, videotape, oral instructions, or a combination of each, in a multimedia format. Also, closed-circuit interactive television, with a picture at both the problem end and the solution end, can greatly increase the efficiency of a computer service call while costing much less than traditional means.

Perhaps the most significant improvement in service businesses of the future will be the employment of streamlined and effective help desks. At the core of the modern help desk will be automated systems that will be very user friendly, flexible, and very clever. These systems will contain a sophisticated contract administration module, which will allow proper entitlement to customers and swift action. Another important feature of the help desk system will be the use of artificial intelligence to diagnose and correct problems. These AI systems will have heuristic, or always improving, features, allowing each new successful piece of diagnostic or solution information to be captured and added to a database of other possibilities. This will enable the user to become more and more proficient as more experience is gained. Special attention will be given later, to these important features of help desks and help desk software and service management systems.

The new service paradigm is suggested in Table 3-1. The significance is that fewer on-site "feet on the street" will be required as service firms solve more calls over the phone, without dispatching. Many service companies are looking to resolve 70 to 90 percent of their calls to the help desk by remote diagnostics and corrections.

By the end of this century, product design will incorporate more redundancies and fault tolerance; it will reduce the size of systems to fractions of their current bulk, as Brainiac, with its 2K of memory, was reduced to the size of a calculator decades ago. Fewer service personnel and more user walk-in replacement or "throwaway" will be the order of the day.

Table 3-1 Changing paradigms for service delivery

Old Model	New Paradigm	Emerging Paradigm
Dispatch	Initiate	User self diagnosis
	Diagnose	Help desk remote intervention
	Solve	Solve or problem bypass
Feet on the Street	Resolve	Solve or swap

As we approach the millennium, the culture shock will be enormous. The authors of this book look at our children and grandchildren and wonder at their facility with the PC; they grew up with it. For us, though shifting technology has become a way of life, it is no less difficult for us to adapt to it unlike the younger generations for whom it is second nature and ingrained in the grade and high schools. A word of caution to readers of the younger generation, however: don't be too smug. Where it took a quarter of a century for technology to reach a point where it boggled the minds of the "baby boomer" generation, it will probably take only a few years for this to occur to your generation. You yourselves will then look at your children as the emerging Wunderkind and will even see an era where your current job has disappeared into source code or been reduced to a summer job for some teenager.

As integration of management tools evolves and more remote, predictive architectures are delivered to the market, service organizations will begin to focus more on business needs and uptime numbers, like the elusive 99.5 percent manufacturing now pursues. Are we seeing the demise of services altogether? Not a demise, but rather a reshaping of them. As service managers and help desk professionals, we will be on the cutting edge of the new services evolving today. Provided we stay on top of our professions, remain current and observant, we will be part of the "New Services" generation; if not, we will be "on the dole" or living with the kids until we find a job (what a twist).

As the pendulum swings in industry we will probably see the reemergence of Industrial Age concepts in delivery of services—for instance, "piece work." An example of this would be in the provision of help desk services from the "home office" paid for on an incident basis. Compensation will be based on calls closed with electronic funds transferred to a value stored debit card.

Chapter

4

Quo Vadis

WE CANNOT AVOID THE URGE TO TAKE AN OPPORTUNITY like this to prognosticate a little about the service business. Back in 1983, when we first predicted a decline in break/fix services revenues, it was such a shocking prognosis that many service managers felt like we had taken a knife and started to butcher their precious cash cow in front of them. However, they soon realized we were "dead" right. Of course, past performance does not guarantee future success, but we have some thoughts on what today's service providers will need to consider if they want to be viable in the next few years.

Perfect Service—from Our Customer's Eyes

Our customers have tolerated service levels that are inconsistently inferior to the improvements made in the hardware and software product areas. While price performances for these products have improved dramatically, our service has barely budged off the standards we set back in the '70s and '80s. We're talking about pricing for value, response and repair times, repeat calls, and DOAs, for example. Customers are tending to desire (and will demand) instantaneous and seamless service. They will be less and less tolerant of interruptions that affect their business. We had better work on ways to do this. Telecommunications, artificial intelligence (AI), and interactive video will play key roles in this pursuit.

Profitable Service—from the Service Provider's Perspective

Providing service to our customers has been challenging, fun, and profitable to some. However, the days of the cash cow for break/fix service are waning. Some of the ways to keep the cash cow alive (or find others in the pasture) entail either increasing revenues or decreasing costs, or a combination of both.

Don't count on raising service prices to increase revenues. Instead, explore, in your own environment, ways to provide *new* services to your customers. Listen carefully to what each customer tells you. (In our stint as a service consultants, the most common complaint service users had about service providers was that they didn't hear what the customer was saying and therefore did not understand the customer's business.) If your customer wants his windows washed, do it! If he wants to outsource his help desk, find him a solution. If he wants a customized service contract, accommodate him.

Reducing service cost is a mountain we all have to climb, whether it's an ant hill or Pike's Peak. Running a service business is very simple: It consists of applying labor and parts to keep the customer satisfied. It's the proportions and nature of each that is the constant puzzle. An oversupply of parts will keep our customers very satisfied but will soon bankrupt us. Too few parts might improve your bottom line, but your customers will "go ballistic." Optimized utilization of labor is also a constant management conundrum. Service organizations need to find ways to improve efficiencies in managing their parts and labor. "How can this be improved any more?" you might ask. "I've been pressured for each of the last fifteen years to lower my costs, and have obliged. I'm running out of ways to pull it off."

A proven way to achieve more productivity in service is to re-engineer it by examining and eliminating useless business processes. Give us half a day with most service providers and we will find at least a dozen processes that cost them money yet deliver nothing of value.

The following list includes trends we see happening in service:

■ *Service engineers changing their roles into service consultants.* The advisory content of service will dominate over the repair activity.

■ *A proliferation of service menus to replace the break/ fix cash cow.* Consulting, network, and software services, self-service, cooperative service, and parts management are examples of newer services to take up the slack.

■ *"Lifetime" warranties.* The extended warranties of some PC products to three years may already be a lifetime warranty since, by the end of three years, the PC in question may be obsolete. This phenomenon is very likely to carry over into other product areas.

■ *"Retainer" service contracts.* An inordinate amount of contract administration results from unbundled service contracts that are a sum of monthly maintenance "box" prices. Elements of the contract may have different terms. Look for newer contracts to reflect a simple, top-level charge, perhaps, annually that states, "For services rendered," with a backup log of date, time, and service rendered. Doctors and lawyers have been doing this for eons.

■ *The change from "help desks" to "management centers."* Management centers will be a brokerage for *any* services imaginable, not just the traditional field/customer/IT services—e.g., sales information, company information, etc. See section 3.

■ *A standard certification institution for service representatives.* Many companies now have certification programs that ensure their customers qualified service delivery. Because of the very diverse nature of multi-vendor customer service, an institution will be established to address common skills such topology, networks, operating systems, etc.

■ *IVDS (Interactive Video & Data Services).* These will function as a set of tools to allow the service provider to respond more capably, quickly, and efficiently. This tool set can involve the customer as well, who, of course, is as anxious to solve the problem as anyone else is.

■ *"No frills" service organizations and operations.* The newer, sleeker service organization will have very few individuals, either management or labor, that are not directly involved with the customer. We will see service managers becoming generalists. Taking part in human resources, long-range planning, technical support, service marketing, training, and many other functions will be shared with service "line" managers.

The list could go on, and will. One change that will not evolve, but should, is a more descriptive vocabulary for *service,* a single word that today means anything from providing a mortgage and flipping hamburgers to fixing your VAX or outsourcing your help desk.

Help Desks Now
The Focal Point of Service

Chapter

5

The Help Desk as a
Solution Broker

Last month, I found myself trying to recover from a head-disk assembly failure. While removing data from the damaged disk, my database was inadvertently corrupted. I placed a call to the technical assistance center. Without their help, these pages would have been corrupted forever.

Two weeks ago, we had a major crisis and found our Accounts Receivable was purged from our system as the result of an error by our software company. We were frantic. Our software company couldn't help us. The help desk spent time on the phone with us and the software company long enough so that we were able to re-create our Accounts Receivable and save our company from certain havoc.

The support center aided me during installation and configuring our Message Router over the weekend, and their help was invaluable.

THESE REAL EXAMPLES ILLUSTRATE THE SIGNIFICANCE AND importance of today's help desks, from the user's point of view. This section will establish a basic definition of help desks and why they are needed. It is intended primarily for those who may not have any familiarity at all with the subject.

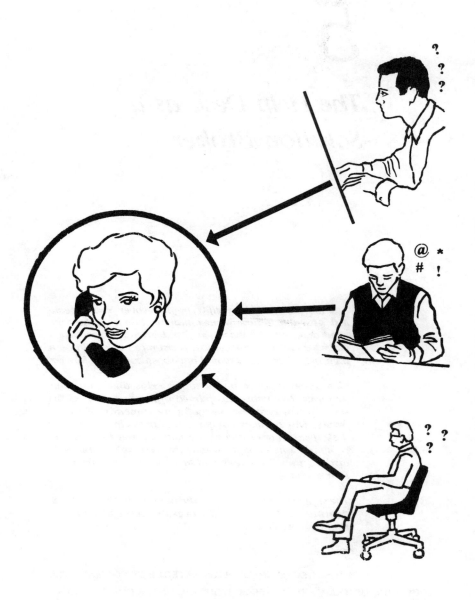

FIGURE 5-1 A help desk is a single point of intervention for solutions

What Is a Help Desk?

Help desk is a relatively new term in the computer industry. In its simplest form, a help desk is a hot line or a place to call if you are stuck, in trouble, or need advice and counsel for operating your computer or for successfully completing a task. "Expert" assistance is usually available someplace either inside or outside your company. It is generally centralized and located at the source of system development. It provides technical and/or administrative support to the computer user. The scope of its capabilities may vary, but, in most cases, the assistance covers hardware and software support, equipment maintenance and installation services, applications and commodity software guidance, and other allied support.

Other terms synonymous with "help desk" include:

□ Call desk

□ Call center

□ TAC (Technical assistance center)

□ Support center

□ Service bureau

□ Hot line

□ *and soon, the management center*

A help desk is a single point of intervention for solutions to problems encountered by users of products and services. Help desks also exist because some users of complex systems would prefer to get the problem resolved by talking on a hot line rather than by reading about it in a manual. And we certainly can't blame them, based on the literary masterpieces created by the vendors. Normally, five to six hundred words in one of the vendor user manuals could be reduced to a single bullet. Is there any debate about the success of such user manuals as *DOS for Dummies*™? Manuals of this type are popular only because they reduce the printed page to an easily read and understood synopsis of vendor tomes.

Problems can arise from the product or service itself, as well as from ancillary products and services, such as a computer and the application software. The problems range from a catastrophic failure where in the end user and his business are totally stymied to a simple question on how to take a shortcut (where operations are not impeded at all). Today, the help desk is usually a broker of solutions, treating the easier problems and passing on the more difficult ones to more sophisticated resources at hand. These resources may be either within the same facility or referred to an outside agency, where there are higher levels of experience with the subject in question. Figure 5-2 depicts the help desk as a solution broker, with some of the causes and effects involved.

A solution broker fixes breaks and finds faults, errors, malfunctions, interruptions, and the like from hardware, software or networks; solves problems that arise from using the equipment, software, or network, such as communications, revision levels, compatibilities, configurations and capacities; Answers questions that go from the idiotic to extremely complex issues such as, How can I join internet from this station?; fulfills a need that exists such as finding a particular program for a user; and fills a demand such as an order entry facility for telephone purchases.

Two Kinds of Help Desks

Internal help desks are strictly inside an enterprise's own operations, and provide a variety of different types of assistance. These centers typically accommodate internal users of the enterprise's computer systems. Virtually everyone within an enterprise uses its systems—even the lawyers! Sales, marketing, engineering, manufacturing, personnel, accounting, and customer services represent some of the functions that utilize information technology in their work. Help desks receive calls from individuals who need support. Typical problems from these callers include questions about applications, for example: "How can I merge my Excel spreadsheet into my Word document?" Or operations: "How do I reboot my system?" Or informational questions: "Where is the nearest CompUSA™ store?"

FIGURE 5-2　The help desk as solution broker

The help desk today is so central to the critical mission of the enterprise that it is ideally suited to take on further roles and additional management functions. The expertise residing in the help desk, along with the management tools that have already been integrated, makes this function ever more useful as a management center. Increasingly, functions such as corporate asset management, HR systems and locators, security, and business operations are being incorporated in this core function.

External help desks provide support to an enterprise's proprietary products outside the company. These help desks are primarily associated with field or customer service operations. Users include companies, individuals, and not-for-profit concerns, who purchase goods and services from the firm that operates the external help desk. Typical callers into the external help desk include users of the product(s) in question, as well as the field/technical service representatives who serve those users. Typical problems involve hardware, software, and network installation, repairs, upgrades, moves, warranty, and information. Often, internal help desks communicate with external help desks, and vice versa, because certain sources of expertise may reside in either place. Figure 5-3 shows the functions of the external and internal help desks. Note that external help desks can also rely on internal help desks for support and vice versa.

Similarities in expertise, tools, and management functions in help desks of larger corporations are getting more visibility, resulting in a restructuring of the help desk function. Redundancies, overlaps, general breakdown of communications, expense, headcount, etc., are all being reviewed with more frequent consolidations of these centers. One large manufacturer recently released an RFP to help desk outsourcers that called for a phased consolidation of more than fifty major worldwide help desks into three or four centers worldwide. The types of centers ranged from internal to external, commodity product support to IT product support, and technical to general business support. This trend will continue at an even faster pace in the next few years.

Manufacturers and software vendors who have external help desks include Lotus™, Novell™, Microsoft™ and Digital Equipment Corporation™. There are thousands of other external help

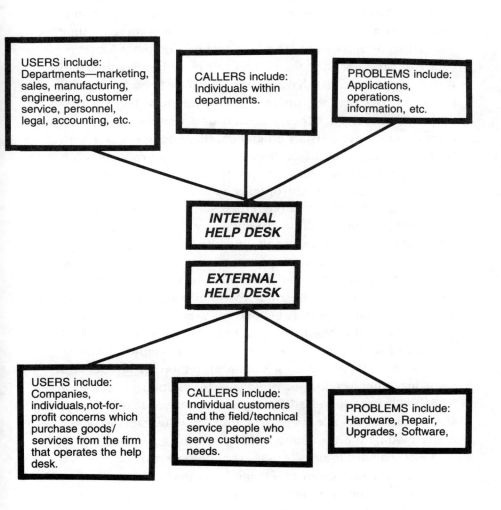

FIGURE 5-3 Basic help desks: external and internal

desks provided by manufacturers and vendors of all sizes and capabilities. The assistance offered by these manufacturers is considered to be maintenance, covered under warranty, maintenance contract, or, if there is no maintenance contract, a time and materials agreement. The aid extended by manufacturers' repair of products they themselves sell provides diagnosis and repair of products that have broken down or become inoperable. In many cases, the primary motive for providing such remote assistance, on either a limited or a lifetime basis, is to increase customer satisfaction and continue open contact with those who have purchased the manufacturer's products. Each call for assistance provides another opportunity for manufacturers to sell new products and options, or to advertise the availability of enhanced systems through their selected market channel. Thus, the help desk can be classified as a "cost of sales" item, which is a definite benefit to the manufacturer.

Help desk resources comprise a virtual supply chain of expertise. Oftentimes, the initial recipient of a technical support call is a local or remote dispatcher who may attempt to provide assistance. If the inquiry is beyond his means, the call may be directed to another resource, which can service several levels of hardware (printer, disk drive or system, for example), software (operating or application, for example), remote or on-site, and involving other vendors or providers. In addition to technical resources, training and administrative assistance may be available within the help desk's organization to aid the caller in better understanding the resolution to his problem.

Help provided internally to users of computers is often more advisory than that given externally by manufacturers. That is, "how to" questions about using the hardware or software systems within the user's computer system or network are answered, but those questions of a more difficult and time-consuming nature are referred to outside resources. Examples of this type of internal help desk are found in large insurance companies, banks, auto manufacturers, all types of franchises or mom-and-pop convenience outlets, grocery stores, and retail stores. The scope of information handled by internal and external help desks is shown in Table 5-1.

Table 5-1 Scope of help desk support

External help desk	*Internal help desk*
Diagnoses trouble	Provides technical support
Initiates resolution	Advises what procedures to follow

Provides maintenance services
   Contract
   Warranty
   Time and materials
	Provides maintenance services
	   How to use systems
	   Password/security
	   Applications
	   Products

Upgrades services	Provides clearinghouse to
	   manufacturers for warranty
	   and service

Sales	Determines internal needs for better training

Teaches callers how to solve
   their problems
	Teaches users how to use
	   applications

Provides customer confidence	Tracks hardware and software "lemons"

The internal user technical assistance center is generally an in-house operation and, in most cases, also acts as the clearinghouse for those break/fix problems associated with product malfunctions. They may have the only personnel who are authorized to initiate a service call to the company's hardware and software support vendor.

Help desks take a variety of calls for a variety of reasons, as shown in Figure 5-4.

If the internal technical support center is centralized, its workload expands dramatically as each new application, new user, or potential problem "creator" comes on line. As demands increase, the need for managing and controlling them is essential. Otherwise, the size and scope of support centers would balloon out of proportion and the whole system would fail. An effective way to nip this catastrophe in the bud is to make certain the support center teaches its customers to solve their own routine problems and to use other "help" resources, including owner's manuals, notwithstanding their complexity.

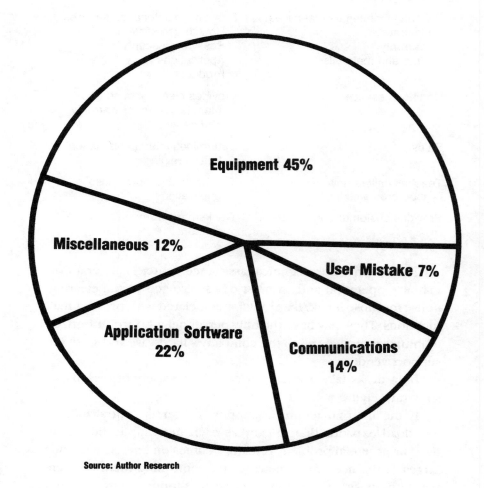

Source: Author Research

FIGURE 5-4 Problems help desks are asked to solve (% of all calls)

Each individual user tends to be concerned only with his or her own obstacle in using the computer. The helper, on the other hand, is democratic and wants to fix everyone's problem, equitably. The number of computer users is increasing every day, and the demand for service and support is becoming more crucial. Help desks accommodate this increasing demand for assistance, but they do not replace the need for system designers and implementors who provide easily understood and operable applications which ensure that users are appropriately trained.

It is estimated that there are well over 100,000 technical assistance and support centers in the United States alone. Many larger companies have multiple help desks. Kodak™, for example, has 70. USAA™ (United Services Automobile Association) has 112. General Electric recently put their foot down and decided to outsource the whole problem of consolidating the multiple help desk entities within their global enterprise.

Different Types of Support

Conceptually, one of the simplest and most commonly used help desks is the directory assistance operator at your local telephone company. In this case, the user needs help in finding a telephone number. By calling 411 or (Area Code) 555-1212 the user gets immediate assistance. Dialing 911 from most telephones gets you immediately to the local police or fire department. The person who answers the phone, under pressure to respond quickly with an answer, must have a systemized way of handling calls for help and resolving each client's problems.

More and more support centers are being installed every day, to the point that the public is growing to depend on help desks for sheer survival. The Internal Revenue Service operates one that advises taxpayers on issues and questions regarding taxes. Radio talk shows can be support centers, too: from his broadcast booth, Boston's Jerry Williams led an influential group that succeeded in rescinding a mandatory law for seat belts. Also in Boston, a night-shift help line was established to aid in dealing with the city's many crises. Called the Night Shift Response Center, it coordinates an array of services from medical to transportation, specifically responding to calls for help made after 5 P.M.

and before 9 A.M. "Re-engineering government begins with basic city service delivery," said Mayor Thomas Menino. "The new system will broaden the city's ability to respond to calls for help around the clock without any additional cost to the city," Menino added. Such emergencies as fallen tree limbs and power outages will be resolved more quickly with the new system. The Night Shift Response Center employs between eight and twelve people working from 3:30 P.M. to 7 A.M.

Recently, my wife started the morning desperately needing help desk assistance; she had locked her keys in the car while the motor was running. On the left rear window was a decal that said to call an emergency 800 number if one should need assistance. She called and got a pleasant and understanding operator on the other end of the line, probably in Detroit. The operator, knowing only my wife's name and address, tracked the Vehicle Identification Number. From there she tracked the key number and called the local dealer at Wellesley-Haskins Olds. Within an hour, the dealer had cut a new key and sent it by taxi to my stranded wife, and she was on her way. This is a brilliant use of a help desk, and will certainly increase our loyalty to Oldsmobiles.

General Electric's™ Electric Appliance Division takes over 3.5 million calls annually at its Answer Center in Louisville. They use a system that includes a massive database containing more than 1 million problem-resolution responses. Any of these can be accessed within two seconds. The center opened nearly fifteen years ago, which shows that the help desk concept is not that new. GE's help desk is just one more example of our society's dependence on help.

The Rising Dependence on Help Desks

The need for help desks is increasing dramatically because of the explosive growth of workstations, desktop, and personal computers in work and recreation. At work, more and more people are doing their own writing, studying, problem solving, creating, and developing while using a simple workstation or

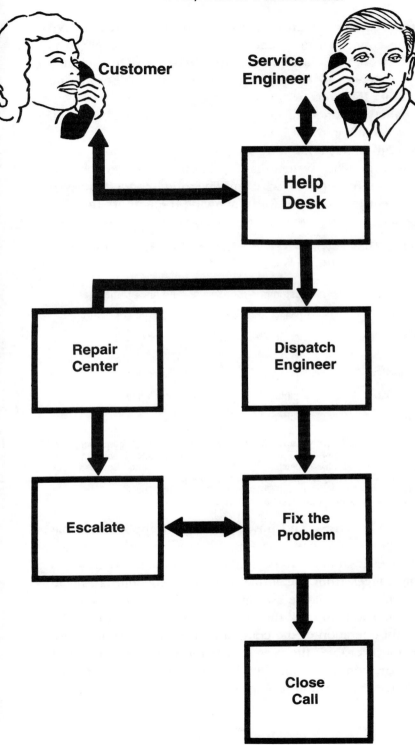

FIGURE 5-5   Algorithm of a simple call flow

desktop computer. A growing number of these hardware systems are connected to a central host system via a LAN (Local Area Network) or a WAN (Wide Area Network). On such networks, messages to Hong Kong, Sydney, Geneva, Tokyo, and many other locations or "nodes" can be sent simultaneously. A wide variety of functions or applications can be performed on this net, including those listed in Table 5-2.

Portions of this book were word-processed on a proprietary, worldwide network system that has 50,000 other users on it. A combination of satellites, wire and fiber-optic conduits relayed the text entries back and forth, allowing the authors the ease and benefits of the large-scale host, without the large-scale cost.

Table 5-2 These Typical Network Applications Require An Internal Technical Support Center

Memo Writing	Customer Proposals	Financial Analyses
Presentations	Spread Sheets	Personnel Locator
Conference Room Scheduler	Sign In/Out Board	Videotext*
Notes File**	Calculator	Calendar
Personal Diary	Training	Stock Trading
Directories	Security	Help

*Library of Catalogs, Industry News, Customer Support, Data and Information Management, Documentation and Literature, Employee Benefits and Resources, Engineering and Research, Financial Information, Products and Services, Job Descriptions and Openings, Manufacturing Information, Marketing Information, Organizational Information, Policies and Procedures, Purchasing, Training
**Interactive discussions of any topic by all interested parties

This comprehensive and powerful array of applications that each computer user has at his fingertips requires expert technical knowledge in order to be able to utilize them. Applications training ranges from the formal classroom to none at all, in which case the would-be user must teach himself through trial and error. The help desk then becomes a critical factor in the successful operation of the computer applications enumerated above and it enables the user to maximize his time and effort when logged on. Technical support must not only provide solutions to user application problems but it must also assure users that the electrical and mechanical operations of the network are problem free.

Help desks for stand-alone users who are not networked usually comprise the hot lines of the individual applications software providers. Individual users may, for example, be stuck using a single Lotus 123™ license and have to call Lotus Development™ in Cambridge, Massachusetts, for support.

As the number of desktop end users who need support grows, help desks become more important in the 1990s. Companies that previously did not use support centers are creating formal end user hot lines, while those with established centers already in place are strengthening their resources. A survey from the Help Desk Institute™ shows that nearly three-quarters of existing support centers plan to enhance their end-user support programs, and more than half will incorporate automated systems to improve their capabilities and allow resource productivity to be increased.

In summary, a help desk is a *solution broker,* answering questions and providing solutions to problems for both internal users and external customers. Help desks are rapidly increasing in number as the number of workstations, desktop, and personal computers proliferates.

Chapter

6

The Help Desk's Goals and Measurements

Customer satisfaction could be improved if customers were given more control over when their problems are fixed. —Gabriel Bitran, MIT™

Every employee must be committed to "going the extra mile" for our customers. Looking back at the gains in customer service, we must build on those efforts to further increase our productivity and effectiveness. —Lino J. Celeste, NBTel™

*T*HESE TWO STATEMENTS OFFER SOME PROVACATIVE messages for guiding a help desk within a corporate environment. An ideal corporate mission statement might state something on the order of "We will provide our products and services to the expressed satisfaction of our customers, creating maximum shareholder value in a cost effective manner, while challenging and rewarding our employees." Service businesses must understand how customers measure quality of service if they are going to meet their expectations and differentiate themselves from other service businesses. The customer will usually base their assessment on *reliability*—do the product and service work consistently when needed? In those instances when the product does fail, the customer will assess the quality of service on how *responsive* vendors are to fixing the problem, the quality of personal contact, and the vendor's accuracy—did he fix it right the first time? In order for you to remain the leader in your market or niche, your customers must be able to differentiate your reliability and your services from those offered by potentially lower priced competitors.

Help Desk Goals

It is possible to enumerate a set of goals in support of the corporate mission. The goals should be aimed at assessing current standards and evaluating current performance in order to achieve new performance levels. These goals might include the following:

1. Define customer-specific service standards for customer satisfaction, service reliability, repair responsiveness, and repair accuracy.

2. Measure actual performance against standards.

3. Empower individual employees or teams of employees to close the gaps and recognize and reward outstanding performances.

4. Determine the major causes of problems and focus resources to eliminate or reduce these causes. Specifically, reduce customer-reported problems by at least 10 percent while keeping costs level, or proportionately so in terms of more equipment to service.

5. Exceed competitor service standards, as measured by competitive intelligence.

Operating Measurements

There are a number of measurements a help desk professional can take to gauge the efficiency of his help desk. They are defined in the following list and incorporated into Table 6-1 below.

Table 6-1 Help Desk Measurement Goals

Operation Goals	Fair	Good	Excellent
MTTA (#Rings)	6+	4	2
InitialCallClosure*	60%	70%	80%
Incidents Logged*	40%	30%	20%
MTTF (hours)	3	1	$\frac{1}{2}$
Escalations*	20%	10%	5%
Automatic Answer*	5%	3%	1%
Hang ups*	3%	1%	0%
Customer Goals			
Response Time (Hours)	4	2	1
Uptime (%)	95	98	99+
Customer Satisfaction	4	2	1
Financial Góals			
Expense** Utilization Rate Direct Labor**	50%	65%	70%

*=percent of all calls
**=Variable

Examples of help desk measurements include:

▶ **Call volume.** Call volume is the number of calls initially directed to a help desk over a prescribed time period.

▶ **Mean time to answer (MTTA).** Mean time to answer (MTTA) is the time in seconds from the first ring of an incoming call to its response by a help desk operator.

▶ **Initial call closure.** Initial call closure represents those calls or problems closed during an initial call between the customer and the help desk.

▶ **Incidents logged.** Incidents logged are the number of problems or questions logged as a result of incoming calls to the help desk. Some single calls may spawn more than one problem or question.

▶ **Mean time to fix (MTTF).** Mean time to fix is the average total time between logging a problem and when the solution takes place.

▶ **Escalations.** Escalations are those problems elevated to a vendor or a backup group for resolution.

▶ **Automatic answering.** Automatic answering represents

those calls that are answered automatically and stored in a call queue.

▶ **Hang-ups.** Hang-ups are those calls where the caller hangs up before being answered by a help desk operator.

▶ **Response time.** Response time is a measure of time between incident and closure. It can mean the time it takes an expert to get back to the person who has the problem, whether by phone, E-mail, facsimile, or it can mean the time between the call being logged to fixing the problem on site.

▶ **Uptime.** Uptime is the percent of time the system is available to users based on a total time period.

▶ **Customer satisfaction.** Customer satisfaction is a customer's overall average rating of service delivery managed by the help desk and based on a predetermined range scale. Data for measurement is most easily collected from a survey sponsored by the help desk or the help desk's service organization.

▶ **Direct labor.** Direct labor is the time associated with the solutions to problems logged from help desk customers and addressed remotely or on-site by technical support personnel. Direct labor measurement can be applied to several parameters such as labor by technician, by problem, by site and so on.

▶ **Utilization rate.** Utilization rate represents the total direct labor (in Hours) expended for a specific period.

▶ **Help desk expenses.** Help desk expenses are the costs specifically incurred by the help desk function including all operations, equipment, and capital depreciation and administrative costs. More detailed measurements might include, for example, cost per problem, cost per technician, cost per site, cost per customer, and the like.

Costs

Exact cost data for individual help desks are fully dependent on the applications, type of assistance provided, breadth and depth of product or technical knowledge, and many other parameters.

Chapter

7

Help Desk Benefits

Productivity

*T*HE GREATEST BENEFIT OF A HELP DESK IS ITS contribution to your productivity or propensity for productivity. By nature, a help desk has a very large leveraging factor on productivity. It is similar to the third-grade teacher who taught us our multiplication tables, or the company manager who nurtures and directs his staff to become better resources for others. It's all about growth and assistance. Productivity is the knack of performing a job better. It is efficiency, and it is measured in gains or losses from a previous or benchmarked period. The Dow Jones Industrial Average is considered a good measure of capitalism's productivity in the United States. If it appreciates over a given time period, it is productive. Help desk metrics, like stocks and bonds, are very simple—dollars and cents—the help desk paying for itself by making users more productive.

Customer Satisfaction

An obviously important benefit provided by a good help desk is customer satisfaction. An unfulfilled need in a customer creates frustration, anger, and sometimes sufficient displeasure to cause that customer to change vendors or suppliers. The antithesis creates the opposite effect: Where customers are promptly, courteously, and ably attended, they are attracted to the source of that competence. An effective support center creates customer loyalty, which in turn enhances the company's or organization's business. Help desks can instill confidence into customers. This is definitely good for business.

For a number of years it has been said that good service is a true differentiator in markets where only a few variables set apart competing products. Customer satisfaction is a state of mind. That state of mind is the result of what users and consumers are used to; that is a function of what manufacturers, retailers, and others in the supply chain make or offer. How willing and how often does the product or service deliverer take into account the customer's unique personal needs? Users' and consumers' tolerance for mediocrity is quite abundant, but good products and services are a sure way to gain market share. It has been proven that those products and services of higher quality are inelastic in terms of cost. People are willing to pay more for quality. A well-functioning support program is a key ingredient in customer contentment and the generation of repeat business.

Credibility

Besides creating a real or perceived state of confidence or loyalty, a technical support center can enhance its organization's credibility in the eyes of the user or customer. A well-planned operating center is the best conduit into the providing firm. It is the face of the rest of the company, represented by a user's view of those people who respond to the telephone. Credibility, like customer satisfaction, engenders loyalty and generates more business.

Picture 7-1   Typical "back room" of a help desk

Improved User Effectiveness

When the assistance becomes more effective, it rubs off on the users and customers. They become more efficient too, and will use less help desk time as they gain individual productivity and confidence.

Job Security

The new support system can provide job security to the initiators as well as to the participants. The emphasis on productivity, downsizing, and re-engineering embodies tools and techniques that are inherently valuable. Help desk staff are key to the whole organization's ability to perform with desktop hardware and software.

In-House Benefits

Many companies are transferring technical support functions to in-house help desks, as the first point of call for employees experiencing technical problems. In-house support staff are often better equipped than outside technical support to diagnose corporate information systems because they are familiar with all the products used by the company and, also, how they compute. In-house support centers can offer a rapid return on investment by increasing end user productivity, freeing more highly trained analysts from routine support tasks, and supporting companywide maintenance and service contracts. In-house help desk benefits also eliminate the finger pointing typical in multi-vendor environments by pinpointing the computer systems that need improvement. (Given the wide variety of hardware and software required to make the system "play" properly, sometimes a vendor will point his finger at another vendor when trouble occurs.)

Help desks also gather information and are in the best position to know what needs fixing in a company's information infrastructure. As a central clearinghouse for problems and solutions, the help desk sees and hears a lot of input and experience, which it can easily pass off to users. The help desk support staff should have a role in determining what gets purchased and what customized programs get developed. The help desk can save money in the maintenance area—an improvement over having each site make its own agreements. The centralized help desk, knowing the overall base of installed products, and having reliability data, can make one comprehensive agreement for personal computer maintenance at a much reduced rate. In-house support desks can improve purchasing decisions and provide information with which to negotiate better prices. Help desks often send out newsletters either on paper or over a corporate network, alerting users to new products and upgrades, providing solutions to common problems, and raising the visibility of the help desk's program.

The challenge to help desks is to satisfy as many and as various needs as there are—a tall order indeed, since the level of expertise of each individual caller can be so different. It is like being an advisor to kindergartners and Ph.D.'s all in one activity. The bottom line is that the increase in productivity and customer satisfaction that efficient help desks can offer amply justifies their existence.

Chapter

8

What Customers Want from Our Help Desks

Common Sense

*C*USTOMERS PHONING YOUR HELP DESK WANT TO SPEND a minimum amount of time answering your questions about the nature of their problem. They do not want to be rerouted to someone else who is going to ask the same questions all over again. Common sense capabilities customers look for include:

▶ *Convenient access* to resources via a toll-free phone number, advanced electronic communications, or public network dial-in.

▶ *Fast response* with 75 percent of all problems resolved within an hour.

▶ *Information, advice, and problem-solving assistance* provided 24 hours a day, 7 days a week, 365 days a year.

▶ *Comprehensive technical expertise* for systems and networks, including those of other vendors.

▶ *A single point of contact* for service.

▶ *Coordinated support* delivered in partnership with *local* service resources, as the help desk may be miles away in a central office.

▶ *Centralized support* where the technical staff provides assistance using conventional telephones, computer-based tools, and network communication.

Support Elements

The modern help desk comprises a number of elements to make it work efficiently.

Remedial support. In the past, if a system was failing or completely down, the only remedial solution was to dispatch a field service engineer to the site to diagnose and resolve the problem. Today, specialists and engineers can use remote tools to isolate and correct many complex technical problems, including intermittent failures, hung systems, and system crashes—often without making an on-site visit. When on-site hardware or software support is needed, however, it should be locally available. And in many cases, hardware problems can be isolated to a specific module, ensuring that the local engineer arrives at the site with the correct part.

Technical counsel. Answers to technical questions must be provided. So must shortcuts or alternative methods for performing a critical procedure or an unfamiliar task. The supplier must be willing and able to conduct research on unique problems of a technical nature.

Problem forecast. Customers can be alerted to potential problems so that corrective action can be taken *before* computing resources or the functioning of the business are affected.

Resources

To offer the responsive high-quality support desired by customers, we must develop a comprehensive concentration of resources.

Personnel. The staff must include an adequate number of specialists and engineers who are chosen for their in-depth technical expertise and problem-solving skills, as well as their customer relations capabilities. Ideal service requires excellent "live person" call handlers. Customers may never need them, but callers get to know names, voices, and unique personal styles that each staff member brings to the job. Technical personnel should be highly skilled and should be able to spend an adequate amount of time learning about new technology and service delivery techniques. A highly collaborative work style should be created. Organize specialists into teams responsible for supporting a family of products or services.

Technical data and information. Help desk staff members should have access to extensive databases that include information on all known technical problems and their solutions. Other topics would include "how-to" suggestions, programming examples, and software product descriptions. All help desks should have their own technical library, consisting of completed documentation print sets and reference manuals for current and mature products.

Tools. Professionals need to use advanced computer-based tools to perform quick, accurate diagnoses of system and network problems.

Test facility. Help desks should be equipped with a test facility where specialists can re-create configuration and problem symptoms. These test beds should include all possible system and network components and the many third-party products, as well.

Product Support

Hardware products are becoming more reliable, but they have shorter lives. An ideal help desk should nevertheless try to support hardware systems and peripherals within its mix for as long as they are in use. All the vendor's current and past versions of software, comprising operating systems, layered products, tools and languages, and off-the-shelf applications should also be supported.

Additionally the help desk must provide advisory and remedial support for all network and communications products so that customers with a service agreement or the appropriate level of warranty can benefit from the totality of resources. Level of access will vary depending on the level of the service agreement, but all customers should be offered prompt, knowledgeable, and friendly support, operating at peak staffing levels during normal business hours. At night and during weekends and holidays, the specialists and managers on duty should be backed up by consultants who are on call to handle unique or difficult situations that require special expertise.

Many help desk owners are seeking to centralize their operations. If you are one of them, there are certain factors you should keep in mind:

Optimum service. Centralizing valuable technical resources, well-trained specialists, expensive capital equipment, proprietary software, and tools can provide optimum support at minimum cost. Obviously, if each and all of these resources were individually dispersed and duplicated at each remote site, the expense would be exorbitant.

Quick fixes. Centralized tools and procedures support fast, accurate diagnosis and resolution of problems. Once the problem-solving process has begun, more than three-quarters of all calls should be resolved within an hour—the time it might take a local field engineer to reach the site if he were dispatched *immediately,* Resolution of 92 percent of all problems should take place within one working day.

Proactive service. Because centralized predictive service tools can identify potential problems, corrective action can be taken before a future interruption develops.

Problem escalation. For a majority of all calls to a central point, the problem can be resolved directly by help desk personnel. When further action is required, the specialist should help coordinate the service effort.

Especially difficult problems that cannot be resolved using centralized resources are escalated accordingly. Some vendors have made significant investments in creating and staffing their help desks, including developing new capabilities for the coming years. Indeed, centralized support is a major component of a long-range service strategy. When state-of-the-art centralized service is coupled with local support that is mobile, knowledgeable, and responsive, the result is a total service solution uniquely suited to what customers want.

Escalation

If at any time, for any reason, the customers are not satisfied with the service they are receiving, they should be able to speak to the manger on duty, who should be available at all times. This manager needs to be authorized to call in special expertise or reassign personnel to a critical problem when, in his judgment, the situation warrants such action. In all cases, a manager on duty should personally apprise the customer of how the situation is being handled.

Coordination

The national or global help desk needs to work in partnership with its local offices. A local office may be asked to become engaged in the situation or problem. The local office may, in turn, need to coordinate its work back to the headquarters help desk specialist. If the specialist determines that an on-site visit is required, he should be able to request that an engineer from the local office visit the site.

The headquarters specialist should then send the local office an electronic copy (facsimile or E-mail) of the customer's service records, including a description of the problem, diagnosis and analysis, and parts numbers for any hardware components that need to be replaced. This message should be received by the local office within minutes of transmission from the help desk. The local office should promptly arrange a service visit, based on the response time specified in the customer's service agreement, and the problem should then be corrected.

Specialists and engineers consult frequently with each other and with help desk consultants, who are among the most senior technical personnel. If a specialist or engineer can't answer the customer's question, he will know where to get the answer. This kind of coordination ensures that the right resources are involved in the problem-solving effort at the right time.

Customer Proficiency

Customers' technical staffs need to be trained and proficient in their computing environment. When they require additional expertise, they can turn to the help desk for information and consultation. As a result, customers' personnel increase their productivity and undertake new projects with increased skill.

Knowledge Base

Help desks gather great quantities of information from their customers and their own personnel. Routinely, this accumulated knowledge is gathered into historical files and technical databases, making it readily available to the help desk's service professionals, who can support their customers more effectively. Customers may also access much of this information, and therefore benefit directly from the experience of others.

Customer Satisfaction

Help desks should be empowered to do what is right for their customers. A satisfied customer expects his vendor to do what it takes to get the equipment back into operation or help complete a time-critical task. In special circumstances, they can provide assistance even if their warranty has expired or the service agreement does not cover the problem at hand. Once a crisis is past, they should make sure that their customers have the right level of service coverage and are properly registered to use help desk resources.

Help desks should make extensive use of computer-based tools and customers surveys to measure performance. The goal is to be the best—and then keep getting better. That means faster response, more accurate routing of service requests, more powerful tools for predicting problems before they occur, closer coordination with local offices, and service that is friendlier, more knowledgeable, and more responsive than can be found anywhere else.

The Art of Triage

Triage is a system used on battlefields of assigning priorities of medical treatment, based on urgency and chance of survival. The television serial *M*A*S*H** incorporated triage in its literal sense. Triage has also come to mean a system of establishing the order in which acts of assistance are to be carried out in an emergency. This definition is apt for managing help desks; triage is a method of providing attention to the squeaky wheel first. A priority system for call handling embodies the triage principle.

Prioritizing Calls

When a call is received, it should be assessed and assigned a priority that relates to the urgency and extent of the problem or outage. Calls are responded to on a priority basis. Response times, escalations, status updates, and call closings are monitored by the help desk personnel.

Urgent Priority. An Urgent Priority call is any call that affects all users on a system, production, or point-of-sales. Urgent calls should be copied to other support personnel for informational purposes.

Response time to the customer for urgent calls should be one hour or less. If the support group assigned to the call cannot acknowledge it within fifteen minutes, the call should be automatically escalated to the next level of support and copied to management.

Escalation of the call should be determined by the extent of the problem and the discretion of management. On-line status

Picture 8-1   The ideal help desk isn't hard to
develop—just ask your customers!

updates should be made whenever the level of progress or support changes and at regular intervals throughout the day. The person assigned to the call is responsible for providing on-line status updates. Ownership of the call resides with the person assigned, until the call is either closed or referred back to the help desk for routing to another individual or support group.

Critical Priority. A Critical Priority call represents a problem call that affects only a portion of users. Response time to the customer should be three hours or less. If the support group does not acknowledge the call within one and a half hours, the call should automatically be escalated to the next level of support, to ensure the three-hour response time to the customer. Continuous effort should be provided during normal business hours and extended hours if deemed necessary.

Escalation of the call occurs as determined by support, or after four hours of continuous effort by any one level of support, whichever comes sooner. On-line status updates should be made whenever the level of progress or support changes and at regular intervals throughout the day. The person assigned to the call is responsible for providing on-line status updates. Ownership of the call resides with the person assigned until the call is either closed or referred back to the help desk for routing to another individual or support group.

Top Priority. Top Priority calls are those that affect only an individual user. Response time to the customer is four hours or less. If the support group does not acknowledge the call within three and a half hours, the call is automatically escalated to ensure a four-hour response time to the customer. Continuous effort should be provided during normal business hours until completion.

Escalation of the call occurs as determined by support, or after four hours of continuous effort by any one level of support, whichever comes sooner. On-line status updates should be made whenever the level of progress or support changes and at regular intervals throughout the day. The person assigned to the call is responsible for providing on-line status updates. Ownership of the call resides with the person assigned until the call is either closed or referred back to the help desk for routing to another individual or support group.

Routine Priority. Routine Priority calls are general requests for such things as file restores from backup tapes, new account requests, software/report enhancements or noncritical upgrades. Response time to the customer is by twenty-four hours, at which time the request should be scheduled with the customer for completion. The call should be referred to a higher level of support if it is required to complete the call.

There is no formal escalation process. On-line status updates should be made whenever the level of progress or support changes and at regular intervals throughout the day. The person assigned to the call is responsible for providing on-line status updates. Ownership of the call resides with the person assigned until the call is either closed or referred back to the help desk for routing to another individual or support group.

Low Priority. Low Priority calls are informational. A best effort should be given to return a call promptly to the customer, because in most instances the call can be resolved with an answer to a question. If the call requires follow-up, it can be scheduled with the customer. The call should be referred to a higher level of support if it is necessary to complete the call.

A formal escalation process should be incorporated. On-line status updates should be made whenever the level of progress or support changes and at regular intervals throughout the day. The person assigned to the call is responsible for providing on-line status updates. Ownership of the call resides with the person assigned until the call is either closed or referred back to the help desk for routing to another individual or support group.

Service Quality

Because service is what help desks deliver to their internal and external customers, the *quality* of that service should be constantly examined for improvements. Most companies can raise their service aspirations significantly if executives take action against mediocre service and set their sights on consistently excellent service.

The sole judge of service quality is the customer. Customers assess service by comparing the service they receive (perceptions) with the service they desire (expectations). A company can achieve a strong reputation for quality of service only when it consistently meets customer service expectations. Knowing what customers expect is only part of the challenge. Another part—a big part—is actually meeting those expectations. What can every company *interested* in improving service do to *actually* improve it? This is answered in terms of five service imperatives:

1. Define the service role.

2. Compete for talent (and use it).

3. Emphasize service teamwork.

4. Focus on reliability.

5. Be a terrific problem resolver.

Customers Show that Service Quality Needs Attention

→ "I was told I would be the first call tomorrow. At 12:30 the next afternoon I called to ask them when their day started."

→ "If you report a problem, they treat you like you have a disease."

→ "There are no standards for quality. We tell them to provide a high level of service to us, their customer, but they don't know what that means."

→ "In their unit, it's sell, sell, sell. And—oh yeah—give service, too. But that's an afterthought."

→ "They have so many rules and regulations that they can't think anymore. They can't bend the rules, or be entrepreneurial. As a result, we suffer."

Service Standards

If management has failed to properly define and reinforce the service role for employees, the result is service role ambiguity (i.e., the concept of service is vague). A potential cause of service ambiguity is the lack of service standards, which are really customer expectations stated in a way that is meaningful to employees. If well conceived, these standards both guide and energize employees and bring a customer focus into the employees' day-to-day service delivery. Managers should consider setting service standards in market segments where the company performance is weak in comparison with competitors.

Management and Quality

Defining the service role is an important step, but it will not get a company very far unless the company has personnel with the attitude, ability, and flexibility to fulfill the role. Two principal causes of poor service quality are placing the wrong people in the service role and giving employees too little control over the service. Services are performances, and most of the time, it is people who render these performances from the customer's perspective. The people performing the service *are* the company.

So why do managers allow the wrong people to carry the company flag in front of customers? Hiring standards are often not based on service standards, contributing to a mismatch between the type of people the company hires and the type of people the company needs to hire to deliver excellent service.

Service managers can add to their problems by not using the full capabilities of those they employ. By using thick policy manuals to control service delivery, managers stifle creativity, diminish the opportunity for employees to grow in their work, and chase the most able employees out the door in search of more interesting work. Thick rule books produce regimented "by-the-book" service, when flexible "by-the-customer" service is needed. While managers are demanding that employees be "robot servers," customers are demanding that they be "thinking servers." Many managers simply do not trust their employees' judgment and make rules to replace it with their own. Able employees are perceived by insecure managers as threatening their control and power.

Service Teamwork

Service work is frequently frustrating and demoralizing. Customers can be rude and insensitive. The sheer number of customers to be served can be psychologically and physically overwhelming. If control over service is dispersed among multiple organizational units that function without cohesion or a unified spirit, it limits the ability of the contact employees to come through for their customers. It is common for service workers to get "beaten up" by the service role, becoming less effective even as they gain the technical experience that should theoretically produce the opposite result. This is "burnout." What customers perceive as inhospitable behavior is actually the "coping" behavior of weary servers who have taken too many punches.

Membership in a team can be rejuvenating and inspirational. To let down the boss is bad; to let down the team is often worse. Team participation can unleash one of the most potent of motivators—the respect of peers. Service teamwork is also important because people in service organizations typically depend on one another. The end service the customer receives is commonly the result of many internal services behind the scenes. Organizational teamwork is clearly not a new idea, but it is an idea whose time has come. Creating the richest form of service teamwork requires long-lasting team membership, fostered by frequent team contact and communication, good team leadership, direction and goals, and a system of team measurements and rewards.

In the latter 1990s, a growing number of service firms will boldly pursue the full benefits of service teamwork by replacing functional organizational structures with market-focused team structure. Management is placing people with different specialities together in the same unit and saying, "Work together as a team, take ownership of the customer, and improve the way we do things."

Zero Defects

Breaking the service promise is the single most frequent way service companies fail their customers. When a firm is careless in performing the service, when it makes mistakes, when it does not do what it said it would do, customers lose confidence in the firm's reliability. They lose confidence in the firm's wherewithal to do what it promises to do dependably and accurately. We sometimes hear executives say that 97 percent reliability is acceptable and that it is cost-prohibitive to do better. The flip side of 97 percent reliability is 3 percent unreliability. More than likely the actual "cost" of 3 percent unreliability is higher than the cost of improving 97 percent reliability. A "zero defects" attitude is as important in service as it is in manufacturing.

Reliability is at the heart of excellent service. No one wants to travel on an airline whose pilots are *usually,* dependable; no one wants to be operated on by a surgeon who *usually* remembers what surgery is to be done; no one want to bank with a financial institution that *usually* keeps its records straight. It is not just the "high stakes" services involving our health or financial security that demand reliability. The dry cleaner that loses our shirts, the automobile repair firm that says a car is fixed when it isn't, the taxi service that forgets to pick us up to go to the airport, the phone company that fails to keep an appointment—these folks cause us to lose confidence in them. The president of a very large telephone company once captured the spirit of a zero defects approach to service when he said, "Think for a moment about what it would mean in our daily lives if people got things right only 99 percent of the time: at least 200,000 wrong prescriptions would be processed every year; there would be nine misspelled words on every page of a magazine; we'd have unsafe drinking water four times each year; there would be no telephone service for fifteen minutes every day."

An important opportunity for improving reliability involves analyzing services for "fail points"—the service processes that are most vulnerable to mishap. Firms can identify fail points by monitoring service delivery through the input of employees actually performing the service; by studying and categorizing customer service complaints (or trouble reports); and by mapping the architecture of the service process.

Outstanding reliability is the foundation on which to build a reputation for outstanding quality. Companies that consider the service promise inviolate are most likely to earn the confidence of their customers. The confidence of customers is the greatest asset a company can have, and can stall the progress of competitors (at least in the short term).

Solutions

When a customer experiences a problem with service, the customer's confidence is jarred but probably not destroyed (unless the problem reflects a pattern of negative experience). What happens *after* the service problem recurs—in other words, the firm's response—becomes a crucial matter. The firm can either make things better with the customer (at least to some extent) or it can make things much, much worse.

Too often, service companies make things worse. There are a number of ways in which they can do this. They set up roadblocks for those who try to resolve the problems. They do not put sufficiently trained personnel, or enough of them, in problem resolution positions. They do not give employees the authority to solve most problems immediately. They do not invest in the communication and information systems that would support the problem resolution service.

Three possibilities arise when a customer experiences a service problem. Either the customer complains and is satisfied with the company's response; or the customer complains and is not satisfied with the company's response; or the customer does not complain to the company and remains dissatisfied. Companies that do not respond effectively to customer complaints *compound* the failure. At this point, the customer's shaky confidence in the firm probably collapses.

How a company handles service problems tells customers (and employees) a great deal about the firm's service values and priorities. There are specific prescriptions for handling service problems:

▶ Encourage customers to complain and make it easy for them to do so. Keep in mind that comment/report cards and toll-free telephone numbers merely scratch the surface of what is possible.

▶ Make timely, personal communications with customers a key part of the vision (strategy). Companies frequently make two fatal mistakes in problem resolution: they take too long to respond to customers and then they respond impersonally.

▶ Answer as soon as possible. Silence is not golden when a problem exists and the anxious customer is waiting to hear something, even if it is only an update.

▶ Encourage employees to respond effectively to customer problems and give them the means to do so. Set up and reinforce standards; give employees the freedom to truly solve customer problems; provide specific training and access to information systems that will tell them about the customers and the situation causing the problem as well as possible solutions.

Managing Expectations

Dealing with customers who want more, better, faster, sooner service *now* is difficult at times. They may seem unreasonable. But sometimes your expectations of them seem just as unreasonable to them. These mismatched expectations lead to misunderstandings, frayed nerves, and frustration. More importantly, they lead to inoperative systems and equipment. But how often do you openly acknowledge this difference in expectations and take steps to manage it? Expectations are difficult to control and impossible to turn off. Understanding the vital role they play can help you improve the quality, impact, and effectiveness of your services.

Some ways to improve your management of expectations include: Guarding against conflicting messages, listening persuasively, helping customers describe their real and perceived needs within their context, and removing fear, uncertainty and doubt. Keep the customer posted, even if you don't have the answer or fix.

Satisfied Customers

Keeping customers satisfied pays major dividends. Customers are satisfied and tend to become long-term customers when delivery of the promised goods or service exceeds their expectations. A "pleased" customer emotionally affirms that your goods and services earn his loyalty. Pleased customers will not move readily to another provider. Creating satisfied customers requires:

- Awareness of the benefits of the product or service;

- Purchasing the right product or service;

- Making the product or service meet customer expectations and producing desired results;

- No major complaints about delivery, price, terms, or performance.

In the long term, however, customer relationships can go wrong. Promises for support are "untested virtues" until proven under fire. Successfully going through a crisis with your customers can cement the long-term relationship.

When products and service meet expectations, customers see service as "good." When they exceed expectations, customers see service as "excellent." They are pleased and will tell four or five other people. When they fall short of expectations, customers see service as "inferior." They become dissatisfied and will likely tell many other people.

▶ 96 percent of unhappy customers will not complain directly to the seller.

▶ 91 percent of those customers will not buy again from that seller.

▶ The customer will tell at least nine people how he "got burned."

▶ 13 percent of those customers will tell over twenty other people what happened.

Telephone Technique

Telephone courtesy may not bring you more customers, but bad phone etiquette will certainly lose them for you. The person who answers the help desk phone represents the entire organization to its customers, be they internal or external. If the caller gets transferred too many times or encounters unprofessional or rude behavior, he is likely to change to a competitor. *Every telephone call that is answered should reflect the message that the caller is a valued customer and that his call is top priority.* Most importantly, the call handler must be empathetic. He must try to put himself in the shoes of the caller and identify with the caller's distress, problem, or question. It is critical to instill good telephone manners in every person at the help desk that comes in contact with users or customers. This is not difficult; it is common sense.

Attempt to answer the phone on the first or second ring. Answer the phone by stating the name of the company and your name. Do not answer the phone while otherwise engaged—in eating, laughter, or discussion with someone else. And smile on the phone. Even though your caller can't see you, put a smile in your behavior and tone of voice.

Never answer by asking, "Will you please hold?" before the caller has a chance to speak. Never put callers on hold without asking permission and without checking back with them frequently to see if they want to continue on hold. Never keep the caller on hold on an open line so he can hear other conversations. Never ask the caller to call back.

Make written notes, including the caller's name. His name can be used again, during the conversation, or when the call is forwarded without having to ask his name again. Address callers as "Sir," "Madam," "Miss,""Mr.," "Mrs." and "Ms." unless you know them well enough to use first names. Note the date and time of the call, the caller's name, his company or business, and his phone number. Include information on the nature of the call, circumstances, and criticality. During the conversation, feed back key points. This shows your responsiveness.

Listen carefully. Never interrupt. You have two ears and one mouth—use them proportionately. Concentrate. Never try to

Picture 8-2   Good telephone skills are essential

do two or more things at once. Give the caller your undivided attention. Never tell a caller "It's not my job" or something similar. Indicate the proper person and transfer the call expeditiously. Take the caller's number and stay with the caller until he connects with the right person. Know what to do in emergencies, including notifying appropriate personnel at home. A designated backup should always be available, on call.

If a caller becomes abusive, try to reason with him. Tell him that you are not part of the problem and hope to be part of the solution—but please calm down. Elevate the call to your manager if necessary, tipping him off in advance, of course.

Never reveal personal or proprietary information. Never hang up first or with a bang. Always call the customer or user back after he has logged a problem or question that has been handled by someone else. Find out, briefly, if the call was closed professionally and courteously.

Finally, if you must use an IVR (Interact Voice Response) system—one that tells you in sequence to "press number two" or "press number one"—make certain it is easy to understand and done by a professionally sounding voice. Don't include interminable loopbacks.

When it comes right down to it, what your customers really want from you is your knowledge. Knowledge and its transmission are the bases of any hot line.

Chapter
9

The Help Desk as a Marketing Differentiator

THE RAPID ACCELERATION OF HELP DESKS INTO THE operations of information technology and field service functions has been precipitated by one factor: the customer. Not only has the customer become smarter and much more aware of both service and the help desk but he demands more from them and has grown to depend on them. In many cases, the customer who uses the help desk of a vendor is also trying to improve his own service to his customers. One firm's service can affect another's business. "Just-in-time" service depends on each link's having a quick and efficient exchange of information and solution to problems.

Service is the ultimate differentiator. Since help desks are a key ingredient of service, they become *the* significant differentiator in a marketplace where common products are separated by the support they provide.

The Help Desk as a Strategic Marketing Tool

Corporate help desks have rapidly changed from a necessary evil, manned by minimally trained clerical personnel, to a significant strategic resource and a critical factor in the initial and follow-on sales of many companies. With the change comes the increased need for help desk staff who are experts and generalists instead of technical specialists. Questions and problems are more complex and range from detailed application development to what to do after a power failure.

Many help desks have met the more sophisticated requirements by employing such things as a CD-ROM database with a decision tree to diagnose, isolate, and address problems. Others who are transitioning from being a reference point for problems have upgraded to becoming a business applications center, dealing with a broad spectrum of issues around the network, PCs, telecommuncations, and software. Centralizing multiple help desks is another important way to meet the more complicated user requirements. Some vendors, especially larger ones, include a customer support center visit and "walkthrough" as part of their executive sales pitch.

Digital Equipment Corporation does an excellent job in using their help desk as a marketing tool. Visitors are greeted by attractive professionals and shown in detail how the customer support center works. As the visitors drive into the support center property, four flags are displayed: the flag of the United States, the state flag, Digital's™ flag, and a flag of the visiting company. The support center presentation usually runs half a day, and visitors leave impressed and confident that behind Digital products is a matchless service and support capability. Digital also distributes an attractive color brochure describing their support centers.

People Helping People

Complex computer equipment and systems require assistance to function. Up till now, this assistance has been of a technical nature. Recently help desks have been receiving more calls for information than for actual technical assistance. The difference is "criticalness."

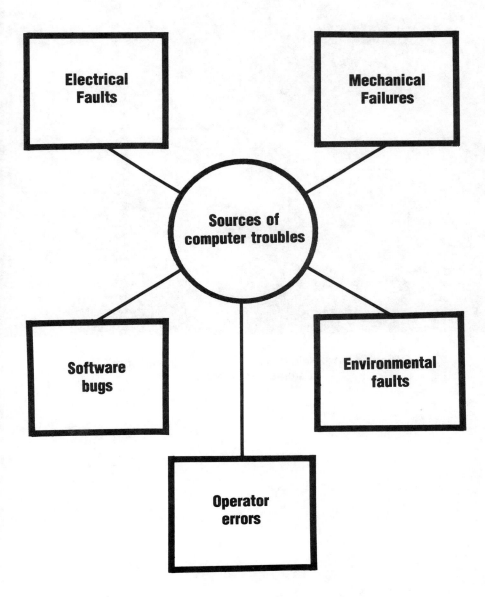

FIGURE 9-1 Sources of computer troubles

Picture 9-1   Help desks like this one make your
customers very happy

Information certainly includes technical material. Given the choice of looking it up in the user's manual or dialing a friendly help desk analyst, most people choose the latter approach because it is usually easier and less time consuming. It is a *lazier* way of finding out what to do. To many people, anything of a technical nature has an aura of mystique about it that creates fear and trembling in the uninitiated. Help desks transform this fear into trust and confidence and lead the user to better appreciation and acceptance of the computer system.

Fear has been known to strike the new computer user. "Oh, I can't use a computer—it's too complicated for me." If the pioneer computer users knew that the machine is only there to enhance their work or life and that there is actually a *human* who can assist them in operating the inanimate tool, there would be more users, especially among senior citizens.

Help desks are about people helping people. It is a *human* voice that usually solves the problem more satisfactorily. There are some artificially intelligent machines that can directly help ailing machines without human intervention, but it is the help desk that assists the people with ailing machines.

The Logic Behind Help Desks

Diagnosis

Just as a golfer examines many ways to decrease strokes, and just as doctors test different symptoms to avoid strokes, help desks use logic and deductive reasoning to pinpoint technical problems and solutions. The faults that computers experience fall into five categories: electrical, mechanical, software "bugs," environmental error, or operator error.

Electrical faults. All computers operate on a simple code using two numbers: zero (0) and one (1). For example, 0100001 means "A" and 01000010 means "B." Electrical energy stimulates the computer on the basis of this binary code, using chips of silicon and metal. An *electrical* error occurs when a circuit in a chip is broken. Today's computers now have self-testing routines

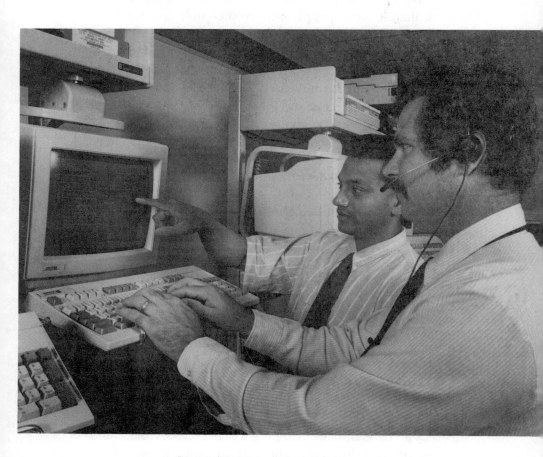

Picture 9-2   People helping people

that can trace the fault to the broken circuit. Fault-tolerant computers have internal diagnostics and comparison logic that can identify a failing circuit before it breaks. The circuit can thus be fixed before the user even knows he has a problem. Electrical problems usually occur on chips located on boards or cards inside the computer and/or peripherals.

Mechanical failures. Mechanical failures occur when a moving part (such as a belt for a printer) wears out. Mechanical failures usually are caused by wear rather than by breakage.

Software bugs. Software bugs create problems that impede the progress of the user. A bug is an unintentional error in the program, which the computer digests and causes it to "get sick." It is fair to say that no software program is ever produced that is completely bug-free. It's a matter of how often the bug shows up and its impact on the work that is underway that determines its magnitude.

Environmental faults. Environmental faults comprise troubles from the outside connection the computer is in, be it a network tied together with telephone lines, satellites, or microwave relay. These faults can also occur when storms knock out power or cause brownouts.

Operator errors. Operator errors are the epitome of the phrase "To err is human." When the trouble is not in the software, or mechanical, electrical, or environmental, it is usually the computer operator doing something wrong with the hardware or software.

These types of faults spawn most of the informational requests to the help desk. The hardware and software products are manufactured separately and operate together only under exact instructions by both. The lazy or hurried user will often call upon help desks when the ultimate solution depends upon facts or instructions already defined and documented in the owner's manual.

Analysis

A problem cannot be fixed if it is not carefully and properly diagnosed. Once the problem is diagnosed, it has to be thoroughly analyzed to ensure that the proper remedy may be applied. There are several alternative remedies for each error, and, again, a decision-tree type of algorithm needs to be worked out before the best solution is attempted. Hewlett-Packard™ made a complete advertising campaign based on the diagnostic and analytical approach used by help desks. It was a program structured around a two-worded question: What if . . . ?

Synthesis

Diagnosing and analyzing problems represent the first part of the ultimate solution. The most important thing to do with diagnosis and analysis is to *synthesize* them into a logical pattern of problems and equivalent solutions. Sophisticated help desks catalogue faults with appropriate fixes so that historical information can be applied to quickly resolve issues. A library of common faults and their remedies is a necessity and can be best accommodated by a computerized database. This database could be as simple as a "symptom/solution" file, or more comprehensive like the "expert systems" now available.

Eureka!

The fix is simply the application of the right remedy to the correctly diagnosed problem. If the potential stroke victim is diagnosed to have occluded arteries, the analysis shows that, among several fixes, angioplasty is the recommended alternative. Other alternatives, as suggested by prior analysis and synthesis, might have included open-heart surgery, a salt-free diet, or other options. But the successful fix is the result of correctly determining and implementing the right logic in diagnosing, analyzing, and synthesizing the problem.

Veterans of field service and help desks have performed "break/fix" services for many years. This type of service still continues; as components break or wear out, they need fixing. Currently, services stress non-break/fix repairs and concentrate more on other aspects of computer services, such as systems integration.

Table 9-1 (on page 91) shows a checklist for solving problems, or incidents, through logical steps.

Date: / /

Fault Details

User Name:	Phone:	Time:

Assigned To

CRC.... USG....	AMD....	Assignee Notified __
TE L__ CSH__	HD __	Assignee Attended __
		Assignee Finished __

Hardware/Software

Device Type:	Device Address:	Media:
Location:	Host Name:	Application:

Problem Description/Action Taken

Reported By;	Date: Time:	Earlier Reference:

Resolution Group/Vendor Action

Actioned By;	Date: Time:	Assignee Reference #:
Handed Off To:	Area:	Name:

Actioned By;	Date: Time:	Assignee Reference #:
Logged: Initials	Time Lost:	Checked By:
Fault Closed Initials:		

FIGURE 9-2 An Example of a Computer Center Fault Report

Figure 9-2 is an example of a computer center fault report, which tracks a problem through the diagnostic, analytical, and resolution stages of an incident.

Valuing and Pricing Help Desk Services

Who is going to pay for your help desk? Most internal help desks today are internally funded, either through a direct budget or by allocations to participating users. This important job is absorbed by the company providing the help service. In some cases the external help desk is also funded by the organization owning it, as a service to its customers. Most external help desks are funded through the warranty or service contract revenues received from customers, directly or indirectly. A new trend is developing whereby the customers pay for the use of the help

Picture 9-3 Diagnostics and analysis are keys to a successful help desk

desk. When we get stumped on the *New York Times*™ cross-word puzzle, we call 1-900-884-CLUE, and for three minutes we can get three clues solved for $1.75. We value this help very much and might pay double or triple this amount, depending on our frustration level at the time.

Two new services are now available with respect to help desks. The first is a computerized bulletin board where, with a modem, you can dial in to leave messages about your troubles and read messages and solutions from others with similar trouble. Another new service is the facsimile machine; when you call a voice-mail number, you will hear a message like "press one if you have a printer problem." This is followed by a detailed fax telling you how to resolve your problem.

Another important trend is the declining price of software. Programs that cost $999 a few years ago are now sold for $99. This puts pressure on help desks. Because workload is increasing but expense is a problem, many companies are limiting free support to the first ninety days.

Major software companies are trending toward a charging scheme for follow-on support. For example, WordPerfect Corporation has many well-trained staff on toll-free lines, backed by "support jockeys" playing tunes and giving updates on when your call will be answered. (This premium type of support has been cited for WordPerfect's success in marketing its cumbersome software.) Now, even WordPerfect feels the crunch and insists you register your program in order to receive support. They will offer support-fee options in the near future.

MicroSoft™ Incorporated is the world's largest software company but is definitely smaller than WordPerfect™ *in terms of support.* After the initial free support period (you have to pay for the phone call), there are several continuing support channels: twenty-four hour recorded or fax back tips; CompuServe™ on-line support; a 900 number ($2 per minute, $25 maximum) voice support; $25 per incident support; and Annual subscription support for $195.

Lotus Development Corporation™ has support that is similar to Microsoft's, although it is easier to figure out which phone number to call. Following the initial warranty period there is a fax-back service and a 900 number at $2 per minute. For an annual charge of $129, you can get daily twenty-four hour, toll-free support for some products.

Borland International™ assigns each buyer a personal identification number (PIN), which every caller must use, good for all products on an unlimited basis. This costs $129 per year. Free support is provided by fax. For $249 a year per product you can speak directly to an engineer. The corporate rate is $5,000 per year for access to four dedicated engineers.

Aldus requires a serial number for service on Pagemaker™. Even then you are likely to leave your name for a call back because of the activity. Of course, if you want faster response by a live technician, you can have it ($2 per minute, $20 maximum). A priority "cut-in-line" service is available for $179 annually. Round-the-clock access is $308 per year. The corporate rate for all products is $1,500 per year.

Staying in Touch with Customers and Users: The Help Desk Survey

The lifeblood of your help desk is your customer or user clientele. If you do not periodically monitor them, at least on an annual basis, for feedback on your services, you will lose touch and compromise all the previous values of the help desk. Table 9.1 depicts a sample help desk survey.

Table 9-1 Example of a customer survey

Dear Customer:
Your comments and feedback are critical for us to maintain and enhance our Help Desk services to you. Please fill out and return this survey.

	Excellent	Good	Fair	Poor
Personnel				
Attitude	[ ]	[ ]	[ ]	[ ]
Competence	[ ]	[ ]	[ ]	[ ]
Empathy	[ ]	[ ]	[ ]	[ ]
Quality of Support				
Solutions/Answers	[ ]	[ ]	[ ]	[ ]
Call Handling	[ ]	[ ]	[ ]	[ ]
Diagnostics Capability	[ ]	[ ]	[ ]	[ ]
Problem Resolution	[ ]	[ ]	[ ]	[ ]
Escalation	[ ]	[ ]	[ ]	[ ]

Comments

_____

_____

_____

Thank You.

Chapter

10

Artificial Intelligence

A BOOK ABOUT HELP DESKS CANNOT AVOID THE SUBJECT OF ARTIFICIAL INTELLIGENCE. Artificial Intelligence is really an oxymoron, though, because any sort of intelligence is *real*, not imaginary, "automatic" or artificial. All intelligence stems from knowledge and understanding and the ability to communicate. Artificial Intelligence (AI) is a "Multi-disciplinary field encompassing computer science, neuroscience, philosophy, psychology, robotics, and linguistics; and devoted to the reproduction of the methods or results of human reasoning and brain activity." As this quote from the *Artificial Intelligence Dictionary*, edited by Ellen Thro, implies, AI means different things to different people. The measure of the success of AI has always been a hotly debated topic. The expectations and relative success of AI in neuroscience or psychology are much different than they are in computer science or robotics.

The *business* interest in AI probably began around 1983, when *Business Week* magazine announced in a cover article, *"Artificial Intelligence, the Revolution Has Begun!"*. This caused quite a commotion in the business community. Up to that point artificial intelligence was relegated to research labs at Stanford, SRI, MIT™ and Carnegie Mellon. According to the magazine article, practical business applications were now within reach. The promise of AI making computer systems as savvy and flexible as human beings, (well, some human beings) was simply irresistible. Businesses rushed to investigate.

By 1984, Security Pacific, Citibank, Chase, Chemical, American Express and other major financial corporations had formed AI groups, or had at least started a project using some sort of AI technique or tools. Most of the initial financial applications involved decision-making systems, including commercial and individual loans, credit card applicant screening and fraud pattern detection. Out of these initial financial projects, three things became clear:

1. AI was not a single, unified solution to make computer systems better problem solvers. Rather it was a collection of decision-making and classification techniques that had evolved out of the university and research labs. Each of these techniques was more appropriate to a particular business problem. Sometimes these techniques could be combined with each other. Sometimes they could be integrated with traditional mainframe systems.

2. To fully realize the business potential of these new techniques would take time and specialized individuals. More importantly these individuals would also have to understand the business objectives driving the applications. This rare breed of AI scientist and technologist who also understood the business side, was hard to find. Expectations and salaries soared.

3. The original AI languages, tools and machines to implement real-world financial business applications were too slow, too expensive, and too hard to understand. The computer languages used to build the first AI software applications were not in as widespread use as COBOL. This made it more difficult to develop and maintain the software. Faster, cheaper and easier tools would have to be developed to allow AI to become a feasible technology choice for businesses. It was apparent that AI was more of a technology *evolution* than a *revolution*.

By 1986 things started to evolve rapidly. On the hardware side, the PC became a mainstream tool. Because of its low price and ease of use the PC democratized technology. It allowed business professionals to explore different AI techniques right on their desktop—*when* they wanted and *where* they wanted. The PC *revolution* was driving the AI *evolution*. On the software side, entrepreneurs developed friendlier AI tools that could actually be understood and used by mere mortals. Modern graphic menu interfaces became a must to any AI development software. No longer were imaginative individuals tied to expensive machines and tools.

Soon small but operational prototypes and applications started to appear and demonstrated the feasibility of artificial intelligence in the business world. Stories of successful AI-driven business applications were published in newspapers and magazines. Many of these stories were the result of journalistic hype, but just as many were true. The American Express Credit Authorization Assistant™, the Coopers and Lybrand's Tax Advisor™, the Chemical Bank Loan Evaluation System, the Manufacturers Hanover Currency Trading Expert System™ and many others were proof of success. In fact many of these AI applications are still operational.

Popular AI technologies used today include: *Expert Systems; Neural Networks (NN); Case Based Reasoning (CBR); Constraint Programming;* and *Genetic Algorithms (GA)*.

Expert Systems

This is one of the more established AI techniques. It has the longest history of proven success. Expert Systems allow storing and applying business "If . . . Then . . . Else . . ." rules to a variety of specific business problems. These include decision-making, classification and configuration tasks such as loan credit scoring, fraud detection and investment optimization. Since the business rules are in English, the prototyping, testing, development and maintenance of expert systems is often made easier than using conventional development and programming techniques. It is also noteworthy that an expert system can explain the reasoning behind a conclusion it has reached, such as, "This loan has been denied because . . .". This explanation capability is extremely important in the auditing and validation of the results of a session. It also helps ensure the system is in compliance with applicable policies, regulations or legal requirements.

Expert Systems can also improve consistency, enforce policy and regulations, distribute expertise to non-expert staff and retain valuable expertise for the company.

Expert Systems are established on a fundamental basis of rules, increasingly refining judgments in activities such as diagnosing a customer's problem or approving a decision to fix a particular problem Expert Systems tend to approach problems from the top down.

Since the rules to be stored in a "Rule Base" or "Knowledge Base" have to be contributed by a top expert in a particular domain of expertise, it is essential that such a valuable individual be available for the knowledge acquisition process. In effect, the knowledge acquisition process becomes a partnership between the business expert and the AI knowledge engineer.

Neural Networks (NN)

Neural Networks (NN) are particularly applicable when a business expert is not available in order to supply business "If—Then—Else" rules, or when these rules cannot be expressed clearly or are simply not known. In such cases NNs can be used to "learn" from historical data bases. The process is not unlike conventional statistical analysis. In effect it is the process of database mining for patterns from existing historical data. These patterns can then be used to categorize or score new data at very high speed.

As it learns, the NN spawns an internal matrix of weights which represent a non-linear relationship between the variables in a specific problem. Once the NN has optimally learned by using database records with a known outcome, it is presented with a set of records with an unknown outcome. This allows testing of how well the NN has learned to differentiate between cases with different outcomes. The learning cycle can be repeated until the system has reached a desired level of performance, or when patterns from new historical records need to be learned and recognized.

Clear evidence of the success of this technology now exists in many fraud detection and credit classification applications.

Neural networks begin from the bottom up, assimilating artificial neurons to create intelligence. Neural Networks try to simulate the brain. Neural Networks are said to be better than Expert Systems because, despite the fact that they both employ patterns for decision-making, Expert Systems cannot handle fuzzy information. Neural Networks know the difference between a handwritten "1" from a "7," and "M" from "N." This selection is learned from experience, the same way we learn as adolescents. Not yet perfected is a neural system capable of distinguishing between "four" and "fore."

Case Based Reasoning (CBR)

This AI technique relies on the similarity of new situations or cases to other, previously solved occurrence. The Case Based Reasoning (CBR) system recognizes these similarities and suggests a similar course of action be taken. For example, a help desk operator fielding a phone call from a user having trouble with a certain piece of equipment, can retrieve from a "Case Base" all previous similar cases based on common descriptions that resemble the present situation. Once these similar cases are retrieved they are further filtered down to fewer cases by asking appropriate questions of the operator. The CBR system can then present the operator with a list of possible actions and solutions that worked in the past for similar cases.

CBR systems allow *problem resolution* without expensive and labor intensive *problem solving*.

Constraint Programming

This AI technique can be effectively used in the allocation of physical or financial resources. Constraint Programming is useful for complex problems that have a large amount of variables which can result in an explosion of combinations when conventional programming techniques are used. It uses specialized pruning techniques to rapidly limit the amount of searching required to produce a solution. The solution derived through Constraint Programming is not always the optimum solution, but can be a very effective solution and will be arrived at in a fraction of the time an exhaustive, conventional programming search would require. Constraint Programming formulas can be used to assign a number of limited resources to satisfy a specific business need, given that in the real world certain constraints and limitations will always be present, and must be taken into account.

Genetic Algorithms (GA)

Genetic Algorithms (GA) and Genetic Programming (GP) are relatively new technologies which are inspired by the Darwinian theory of evolution. A population of individuals, each representing a possible solution to a problem, are initially created at random. Then pairs of individuals combine to produce offspring for the next generation. The system is run for dozens or hundreds of generations. Because the probability of an individual reproducing is set to be proportional to the goodness of the solution it represents, the quality of the solutions in successive generations improves "automatically." The process is terminated when an acceptable or optimum solution is found, or after some fixed time limit.

GAs and GPs are appropriate for problems which require optimization with respect to some known criterion. These technologies can also be used for classification problems where data is available but good classification rules are not known.

For GAs, problem solutions are coded as long binary vectors, called chromosomes, which are merged and permuted in the reproduction process.

For GPs, a solution is represented by a tree structured LISP program. Random subtrees of the two parents are exchanged and permuted to form the offspring.

An advantage of GA/GP is that it is not necessary to know in advance *how to solve* a problem; it is only necessary to know *how to rate* potential solutions. To apply the technology it is necessary to write an evaluation function and a function to code solutions. These functions are then called by the standard, existing genetic system. Consequently, working prototypes can be developed in as little as one week. A disadvantage is that the technique is very computationally intensive. For complex problems the system may need to run for many hours or even days on a PC-class computer. Large, complex problems may require the availability of a fast workstation-class computer. AI techniques and tools have evolved to a point where they can help businesses develop more effective products and processes, and deliver more effective services.

We would much prefer to use the term "Computer-aided Intelligence," (CI) instead of "Artificial Intelligence," because we enhance our intellect by designing and implementing tasks with the computer, and the result is not "artificial." This enhanced knowledge may not have been feasible using the human brain alone. However, this is not meant to be a sermon or debate about what artificial intelligence is or is not. Rather, we need to understand where this "computer-aided intelligence" fits in with service and help desks.

First of all, it can safely be said that computer (and other) service is knowledge-intensive. It takes a great deal of know-how to fix complex bugs and faults in systems. If this learning can be accelerated by "computer-aided intelligence," then problems will be solved faster and better, and the customer will be happier. If, then, we can accept the empirical definition of artificial intelligence as 'computer-aided learning or intelligence," then the most important thing to do next is to see how it can help us and our customers. A help desk can use CI (Computer Intelligence) to facilitate handling a customer problem and reaching a swifter and more reliable solution. This aplication of CI comprises different databases and systems to deliver immediate expert knowledge to the user and thereby successfully diagnose and fix customers' problems at the first attempt.

Reliability data from completed service activities can be used with self-improving algorithms to interpret the relationship between problems, symptoms, diagnoses and actions, as well as parts used. An understanding of the working environment is built up and constantly refined as more data becomes available. The CI system will detect and project patterns of problem trends and the most successful "fix" strategies. Such a CI system can give service managers fast, accurate, on-line access to details of problem patterns and trends displayed by products held within the database, to analyze engineer behavior and to confirm that known problems are under control.

Call handling systems create a wealth of information which can be utilized in CI knowledge databases. CI can provide information about common problems in products and help management anticipate the parts and labor resources required for restoration. The source data for a CI help desk system can be extracted automatically during the normal call-completion process. Use of existing integrated service knowledge, collected routinely during normal work processing, eliminates the usual issues and costs associated with the use of knowledge experts who are needed to establish a situation rule-base. The database is updated in real time for every new occurrence of an existing problem, as well as new problems.

The CI system can display likely causes of a problem which is reported for any specific product. This allows relatively inexperienced help desk personnel to screen out those expensive labor intensive calls and refer then for proper handling. Where a service visit is required, the CI system can provide accurate prognoses about typical fixes, repair times and probable parts requirements during the on-site call. More first-time fixes will enhance customer relations and employee job satisfaction.

A CI system can provide service management with product reliability facts, indicating the need to improve training of service personnel and front-line help desk staff, as well as optimizing parts stocking levels and/or resource requirements.

A CI service system can also provide a unique opportunity for manufacturing functions to adjust manufacturing processes for improved product quality, reliability and serviceability.

By checking historical data held in the CI help desk system personnel may gather service histories for a particular item relevant to a particular problem. Common causes of reported or suspected problems can be listed according to probability, and updated in real time as the help desk operator continues investigations to discover new problem resolutions.

An experienced technician can usually diagnose and fix problems but it is impractical to employ individual experienced in help desk support. CI can turn call handlers into proficient help desk operators through the use of expert systems facilities which increase their available knowledge about problem resolutions, using statistical reasoning techniques. This has improved productivity by eliminating the need to send skilled servicemen on-site. The operator now recognizes these as often avoidable on-site calls.

The CI system can produce a likely diagnostic list, ranked by probability, for a given mixture of product and reported problems; together with estimated time required on-site by servicemen to complete suggested actions, and the anticipated parts required to successfully fix the problem on the first visit. This knowledge is invaluable to less experienced personnel who can help eliminate unnecessary on-site visits.

The CI help desk system can provide detailed managerial reports identifying the pattern and trend of problems by focusing on faulty products and questionable spares. Excessive numbers of normal and high value parts on ranges of products can be useful for stock level analysis, costing maintenance contracts, and to identify costly or wrong corrective actions. Anomalies identified by CI parts usage reports can be used to inform individual servicemen about the most (and least) successful repair records. Bad product batches or impending obsolescence can also be determined by isolating problem trends within the database and indicating problem patterns in call rates and parts cost.

11

Planning a Help Desk

Selling a Help Desk Internally

*T*he prudent help desk sponsor will begin his plan for obtaining and implementing a formal help desk system months ahead of the targeted need date. Part of this approach is to plant a seed by briefly describing the help desk system to the person, department, or organization that will be funding the help desk, using an educated estimate of its cost, as early in the budget cycle as possible. Company policies and procedures should be thoroughly researched to determine the right way to proceed. Questions regarding the appropriate budget—capital or expense—may be answered in the company's financial guidelines. Pro forma budgeting processes often accommodate and/or precipitate preliminary planning and dialogue regarding new items to be budgeted or considered for budget. Normally, enough time is allowed to refine the specific cost justification details and description before any decisions are made. Major budget appropriations or expenditures do not always survive the initial request phases. Perseverance, however, may pay off.

The ultimate sponsor of the help desk system is usually the head of field service or field service operations from the *external* perspective; and the manager of information technology on the *internal* or user side. This person must be prepared to spend a significant amount of time and energy fighting for the system he knows is able to do the job now, as well as in the future. Having already invested several weeks in planning and designing help desk systems, he needs to spend additional time drafting a business case.

An initial draft of the business plan can usually be obtained from the preferred systems vendor. The plan, minimally, must include the following:

— A complete description of the system

— Features and benefits

— Organizational impact analysis

— Cost breakdowns and options

— Implementation strategies

— Selection criteria

— Return on investment analyses

The plan should be prepared in a format that is familiar to top management and other decision makers and recommenders. An informed consultant can be strategically employed to help put the plan together, including the system selection process, if circumstances permit. Otherwise, it is most politic and wise to include in the planning process as many internal members of the organization, including users, as possible.

Throughout the process of planning a help desk system, initial budgeting for it, and building a fail-safe business case, the sponsor/author should strategically involve various influential personnel who will have a stake in the system either by paying for it, implementing it, or using it. Typically, these include representatives from the service function and the information systems function who have to set up, operate, and maintain the system among all the other in-house and vendor-provided programs. Also on the "team" are members representing the executive level of management, including those holding the company's purse strings. Not the least significant team members are users and field engineer representatives, as well as the dispatchers, call handlers, engineers, and technicians who ultimately will be required to use the selected help desk system. The task is to mold the team into a unified, deliberate, focused, and persuasive group. When the business case is finally presented for approval, members of the team should share in the presentation. One or more dry runs are recommended.

Many highly motivated managers fail to translate a conceptually sound help desk scheme, for improved and more cost-effective operations, into a successful reality. Too often this failure is a result of lack of support from upper management. To succeed with an undertaking as major as a help desk system, the sponsoring organization needs the full support of plant and corporate management. Developing a sound help desk requires the commitment of many resources, including in-house devotees and outside consultation with other professionals to ensure realism and acceptance. Many man-hours and dollars will be expended before measurable results can be achieved. Because problems will arise along the way, management needs to be solidly behind the program while it is being put into place.

Failure to get approval for a help desk project results from several things, including lack of credibility in the help desk manager, failure to understand upper management's perception of the economics involved, failure to establish priorities as management views them, and lack of clarity in presenting the steps for establishing the help desk. When the sanction of others is sought, persuasion dynamics are important. Credibility will probably be the most important factor in determining whether a project gets approval. This helps to explain why one manager will go in with a well-prepared presentation and come away with nothing, while someone else makes a few suggestions and gets the approval to go ahead.

Another consideration in selling a help desk project is realizing that the manner of presentation may be more important than the content. The presentation should include the steps involved in developing and implementing the desired program, a realistic assessment of resources and efforts required to make it happen, and an appraisal of expected benefits. Each part of the presentation needs to be prepared carefully. The steps involved in making a help desk system work are fundamental.

Determining which resources are required is more difficult, though they are simply a best estimate of the people, time, outside help, and expense involved in each step. If no one in the organization has been fully involved in instituting a help desk project, the sponsoring manager may want to talk with people in other companies who have established such a program, or consider receiving help from a consultant.

Identifying the expected benefits from a help desk program or system is crucial to getting approval. Without a return on investment, why would a top manager be interested? The help desk manager, assuming that not everyone knows why the program is important, will want to have all the facts handy so that he can emphasize the benefits. The manager should demonstrate his confidence in his program and should not be afraid to ask for what is really needed.

Building a Help Desk from Scratch

Your objective in starting a help desk from scratch is to free up engineers and others to make them more productive without compromising attention or service delivery to the important customers or users who rely on your organization's help to do their jobs. Figure 11-1 shows you the elements you will need to start your own help desk.

Blueprint This detailed plan is a flexible guideline for major milestones in the development and implementation of your help desk. This would be a tactical, working document, that includes a time line, to clearly define, modify, and expedite project activities.

Call flow. Call flow should be based upon the most efficient methodologies of logging, handling, and closing calls within your unique environment.

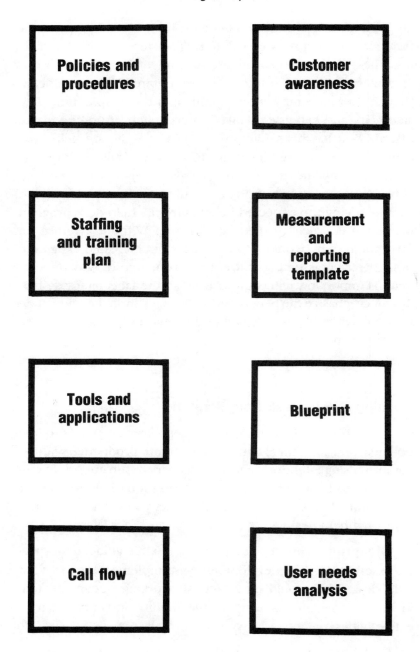

FIGURE 11-1 Building a help desk from scratch requires these elements

User needs analysis. This analysis should be purposely biased toward the real and perceived requirements of your customers. Customers or users should be carefully sampled to determine a representative configuration of needs. This is an important factor in building your help desk. Experience shows that respondents are very comfortable and candid with this approach, which makes them feel like participants in the new procedure, as opposed to having it jammed down their throats.

Staffing and training plan. A plan for training and manning your help desk is crucial. Technical training from your engineers or technicians will be important. Staff can be outsourced.

Measurement and reporting template. Realistic and meaningful goals and reports need to be addressed and designed. By properly capturing call data, a fault/fix library can be built to handle calls more productively.

Tools and applications. The plethora of help desk management software can be overwhelming, confusing, and extremely time-consuming to appraise. Consultants can provide you with an existing, predetermined analysis of several of these and assist you in developing a short list of potential vendors. They can also help you in determining appropriate space arrangements for telephone and other office information equipment.

Policies and procedures. A brief but comprehensive set of help desk policies and procedures to incorporate your unique operational standards should be documented.

Customer awareness. You need to"train" your customers to use and support the new help desk and to reduce their natural urge to continue calling engineers and technicians directly.

An experienced help desk project manager should be assigned to develop a help desk project plan, to schedule major events and provide project direction. The project plan is a statement of all major components of the help desk solution and how they contribute to solving users' requirements. The project plan is complete only after all related technical and business issues have been identified and addressed. A kickoff meeting should be held as soon as the project manager believes that most of the critical areas have been identified and resources have been assigned. The purpose of this meeting is to establish mutually understood (team) goals, additional team requirements, and the overall project schedule. In addition to identifying internal resources, the project manager needs to identify specific sources for information related to help desk users so that the best possible understanding of users' needs is being incorporated into the resultant operation. When all users have been identified, a knowledgeable and capable representative from each user group should be requested to participate on the project team.

Figure 11-2 shows the parameters you will encounter in developing your help desk project plan.

Each parameter has its own data requirements, that is, the information you will need to plan your help desk. The following tables detail the minimum data requirements for each of the parameters in Figure 11-2.

Tables 11-1 through 11-9 describe much of the information needed to plan the help desk.

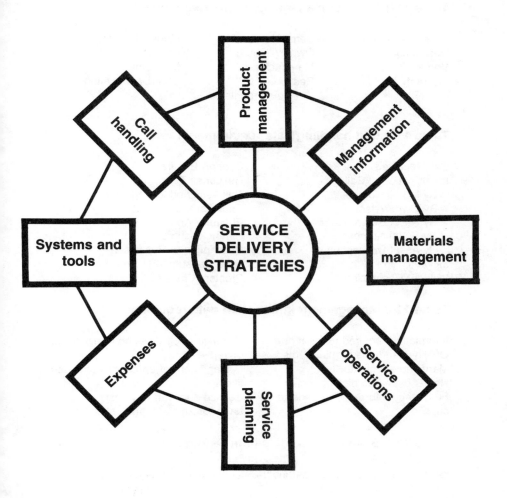

FIGURE 11-2   Project planning parameters for help desks

Table 11-1 Product management data requirements

Asset Reference	Serial Number	Model Number
Description	Owner/User	Location
Vendor	Manufacturer	Maintainer
Warranty	Response Requirements	Cost/Depreciation

Table 11-2 Call handling data requirements

Call Received	Support Engineer
Identification of Call	Response Time
By Model Number	Call Assigned to Engineer
By Owner/User	Engineer Dispatched
By Asset Reference	Engineer Arrived
By Serial Number	Parts Consumed
By Asset Description	Description of Resolution
Incident Type	Time Consumed to Resolve
Incident Description	Problem Closed

Table 11-3 Management information data requirements

Information required to meet needs	Historical activities no longer required
Quality standards requirements	
Management capability	Management of operations (call activity)
Needs based on discrepancies	
Frequency information needs to be supplied	Service and warranty costs
	Labor productivity and utilization

Table 11-4 Systems and tools data requirements

Labor activity reporting methodology/process	Cost (direct/indirect) allocation and recovery systems
Personnel system interfaces	Documented personnel policies and procedures
Hours worked reports and data acquisition processes	

Table 11-5 Service delivery strategies data requirements

Maintenance philosophy by product type, e.g. Field replaceable unit repair or replace, return to factory	Diagnostic methodologies
	Support philosophies
	Escalation procedures
	Levels of support

Table 11-6 Materials management data requirements

Materials purchases process
On-hand (quantity, value) rules/ guidelines
Scrapped/obsolete process
Expendable materials management process

General material tracking systems and processes
Repair processes and their interaction with service units

Table 11-7 Expense data requirements

From an historical perspective (budgets/actual, etc.)
With relationship to individual business units
With focus on differences within specific geographic units
Labor costs and control
Travel costs and control
Training expense and control

Repairs and associated expense (freight, etc.)
Materials
Warranty expense and management
Overhead (general and administration)
Miscellaneous expenses

Table 11-8 Service planning data requirements

Service delivery methods and procedures
Service technologies and implementation
Vendor interfaces
Service quality controls

Service product introduction
Service reporting
Service method or procedure change process
Subcontracting

Table 11-9 Service operations and management data requirements

Call handling (fault recording, dispatch, management)
Problem management and problem excalation
Service operations infrastructure and its suitability/ability to adapt to changing needs
Service operation productivity

12

Most Critical Problems in Running Help Desks and How to Solve Them

YOU ARE SURE TO RUN INTO A NUMBER OF problems in running your help desk. They can be divided into two major categories: operational problems and organizational problems.

Operational Problems

Financial performance. The average help desk has a poor record of its own costs and, where applicable, revenues. This serious problem manifests itself in several different ways that are not beneficial to the help desk. The absence of financial information makes it very difficult to request additional personnel, for example. How can added personnel be justified without at least a cursory financial statement? How is the value-added of a help desk employee measured? Another negative manifestation is the lack of management interest or involvement with help desks. Unfortunately (or maybe, fortunately) executives seem to spend their time in areas where the flow of money can be closely monitored and controlled. A help desk without financial responsibility is a sure candidate for executive avoidance.

Accountability.   There is an alarming problem that is pervading some of our major businesses today. It is lack accountability. As many organizations reengineer their work and processes, the result is often layoffs or buyouts. Employees are responding in some cases with not only a lack of loyalty but also an attitude of letting others take responsibility. Our corporate society seems to accept this lack of accountability. The help desk is not immune. The process in most help desks involves handing off the customer's problem to an expert or series of experts. This process often leaves the loop unclosed, with service calls that are never closed.

Unclear direction and goals.   Help desks seldom have a clear charter and strategic and tactical goals. This is one problem that makes the help desk hard to monitor in terms of successful performance. Tactical goals such as those mentioned in chapter 5 need to be implemented.

Records quality.   Inaccurate records plague most help desks, especially those without automated systems. Many mistakes are made in the transfer of information. The more handlers of a caller's problem, the more inaccuracies as information is passed from one function to the next.

Archiving.   There is always a question of what data is no longer useful or valid and when it should be extracted from the working database. The analogy here might be teeming file cabinets with useless and outdated information. Some of us have had the experience of throwing some of our files away, only to need them later and not be able to find them.

Systems/Linkage.   Help desk systems are often standalone systems that do not interface with other important systems in the help desk firm. This lack of integration can create a significant impediment to the company's operation and financial performance.

Independent systems.   A corollary to the Systems/Linkage problem is the problem that too many independent systems exist in a help desk environment. Many of these are product based instead of customer focused.

Customer interface. This problem includes the voice and attitude that the customer listens to when he calls for assistance. Busy signals, queuing of calls, and unpleasant call operators present an unprofessional picture to customers who have problems or whose questions are critical. One of the most abusive traits of help desks is to dictate when service will be provided without asking the customer when they would prefer to have the service performed.

Internal communication. Weak feedback links between workforce, management, and the help desk are prevalent. As a result, commitments are made without knowledge of help desk management.

Network alarm. A significant number of many help desk network systems do not provide alarm status. Alarm/fault correlation to affected customers/services are difficult to provide.

Tools and methodologies. Help desks have a tendency, like the proverbial shoeless cobbler, to lack the necessary tools and techniques that would enable them to do their jobs properly. For example, there is a growing number of commercially available artificial intelligence tools for diagnosing problems. In fact, though, very few help desks employ this technology. As to methodologies, help desks can treat the same problem with multiple solutions, or they can treat multiple problems with the same solution. But the lack of techniques and methodologies to perform diagnostics and solutions, result in inefficiencies.

Point of contact. In larger companies, where numerous product lines exist, it is common to have a service number for each product. At times customers do not know whom to call for particular service problems. Furthermore, there are usually too many people involved in the process.

There are, of course, many other different operational problems within help desks. The few mentioned above are samples and are representative of those with which the authors are familiar.

Organizational Problems

Staffing and training. There are no formal training or vocational schools available for help desk personnel. Therefore the staff at the help desk is usually pulled from the ranks of the company because of expertise and talent with respect to handling customers, knowing the technical side of products, or having specific vendor or multi-vendor skills.

Career path. A major problem affecting all help desks seems to be the issue of how good performers in the help desk function get rewarded, in terms of advancement and promotional opportunities. Because of this, the help desk has difficulty in attracting motivated workers in the first place.

Burnout. The help desk job is very similar to the emergency room at hospitals—it is filled with pressures and problems and takes its toll amongst its employees.

Management indifference. Company executives are often indifferent to the help desk and do not realize the important role it plays with the customer base.

Answers

As Larry Glick of WBZ™ Radio in Boston used to say, "I'll always give you an answer—I'm just not sure it's the right one." There are several improvements or answers to the aforementioned problems that should be considered. Perhaps the first important "answer" should be to differentiate your company through quality of service. This should involve a move toward zero defects from a customer perspective. The reality is that it is prohibitively expensive to make every product with 100 percent zero free defects. However, the harder we try for this the more customers we will attract. Help desks need to be more responsive to customer needs, cost effective, aware of employee contributions, and integrated in terms of network information management and repair capabilities. Help desks also need to:

☐ make it easier for customers to complain and learn how to avoid similar complaints in the future

☐ understand customer needs that are customer specific instead of service level oriented

☐ know their customers, keeping information on their needs and what they currently provide them

☐ know and understand competitors' service levels

☐ respond quickly to customer troubles

☐ take ownership both as individuals and teams for customer problems

☐ communicate and share information

☐ provide high-quality, personal contacts with their customers

☐ provide incentives for customer involvement in the service process

☐ minimize network rearrangements

☐ aggressively deploy state-of-the art technology to create a more responsive process

☐ bring information and testing capabilities closer to the customer

☐ solve problems at first point of contact

The single most effective approach to solving the problems of the help desk is to establish or enhance its goals and objectives. By articulating the job of the help desk in this way, the help desk will gain the respect from executive management that will be the instrument that helps it add more people, get more tools, respond to customers better, etc. By getting management involved and interested, many of the problems will disappear.

My wife works at Rizzo Associates™ a very successful environmental engineering and consulting company, which has had recognition in *Inc.* magazine. The president, Bill Rizzo, makes an offer every year, to promote the United Fund, to exchange jobs for one day with the highest bidder. Recently that person happened to be on the company's switchboard, which is not unlike a help desk in receiving customer calls for help. Bill took over the operator's job and salary for one day, and the operator took Bill's salary and job for the day. This ended up being a truly eye-opening experience for the president, who got firsthand knowledge of how his customers were faring. This would be a good idea for many presidents to follow.

Chapter

13

Staffing and Training Help Desk Personnel

Staffing

*H*IRING A GOOD HELP DESK TEAM AND KEEPING THEM
motivated is a common concern amongst most support operations. It is important to fully communicate job descriptions, performance expectations, pay ranges, and career paths. Regular
analysis of calls received can help determine any changes in staff
size and skill needs.

To ensure a successful help desk, make sure the staff has the
correct skills and personal characteristics to match the main
functions of the help desk. Also make sure that the personnel
assigned to the help desk have basic skills for interacting with
users and accurately communicating information to the support
staff. The help desk staff should include specialists who have
the skills to handle problems in one or more specific areas, such
as hardware, software, networks, or specific applications.

The following sample position descriptions describe the es-
sence of help desk work in a computer environment.

Help desk manager.   This person is responsible for the overall management of the help desk operation. This includes, but is not limited to, the allocation and assignment of help desk resources, development and evolution of the operating plan, development of operating budgets, and actual service delivery. The help desk manager is also responsible for development and management of second-level support agreements, management reporting, customer interacting, managing and escalating serious problems and measurements. Also included are the introduction and the support of new products, services, and users, marketing the help desk services internally to management, and monitoring and improving the operations. Developing, communicating, and renegotiating level of service agreements, managing conflicts, and representing his company to the customer are additional responsibilities.

Customer liaison.   This resource is responsible for providing first-level problem management to users. Responsibilities include answering telephones and users' questions, documenting problems, logging calls, tracking problems and providing status, searching databases for solutions to problems, escalating problems to management, and inputting solutions into databases.

Associate hardware specialist.   This specialist follows established procedures and standard guidelines and performs routine technical duties involving testing, troubleshooting, identifying, and isolating faulty components in the repair of computer systems for a medium range of products. He performs option or simple system checkout to ensure proper equipment performance to meet standards and customer expectations. He isolates and resolves malfunctions and utilizes higher levels of support for any nonroutine problems.

Hardware specialist.   The hardware specialist responds to issues such as hardware malfunctions, site audits, or installation calls and may evaluate environmental conditions to assess potential causes of problems. He utilizes higher levels of support as needed. He researches problems and provides or coordinates solution. The hardware specialist maintains contact with problem situations and assists until satisfactory resolution is achieved.

He assists occasionally on product performance or service delivery improvement methods. He works with limited supervision on customer problems as assigned, exercising discretion in defining and solving technical problems where alternative choices may be applicable within standard practice.

Senior hardware specialist. He responds to complex, unusual, intermittent, or undefined hardware calls; researches problems and implements solutions; monitors problem situations and, if necessary, involves product vendors; and consults with management on technical issues related to improving product performance, service, and delivery procedures. The senior hardware specialist also conducts technical product performance improvement projects, and develops service delivery support methods and service tools. He directs the activities of other support engineers and exercises broad discretion in defining and solving technical problems where alternative choices may be applicable within standard practice.

Associate software specialist. He provides basic software support for customers; resolves routine problems on selected products; and refers nonroutine problems to more senior specialists. Training may be required as selected products are added to responsibilities.

Software specialist. The software specialist participates in either the development, testing, documentation, and maintenance of simple software programs and parts (reports) of sophisticated systems or is responsible for training. He implements projects of limited scope and complexity. He performs design and analysis tasks of a limited scope and complexity and works on problems that are well defined; that is, factors or other data that are specific and point directly to the problem. Typically, problems are a subset of a larger issue, and are frequently repetitive.

Senior software specialist. He performs design, development, testing, documentation, and analysis on complex programs, sophisticated systems, and databases. He works as part of a project team or as a leader of a defined section of a major project; establishes reasonable and measurable scheduling milestones; conducts design reviews; and provides status reports on project. He develops functional specifications, and may recommend changes to existing specifications. He solves problems involving very complex technical issues across multiple disciplines.

Associate network specialist. He performs operational and analytical activities to provide for maintenance of Local and Wide Area Networks data communication. He assists more senior support in identifying network needs and requirements. As assigned, he performs basic analysis and recommends solutions to basic networking problems given close direction.

Network specialist. He performs and coordinates operational or analytical activities related to the implementation, operation, and maintenance of Local and Wide Area Networks and related products. This may include alarm monitoring, traffic report analysis, system restarts, and system configuration/parameter changes. This position requires the ability to analyze, develop, and implement solutions to network problems of moderate complexity, regularly exercising discretion and independent judgement. As a member of a team, the network specialist helps develop network solutions to complex projects. He functions under general supervision.

Senior network specialist. The senior network specialist provides technical direction for operational support of Local and Wide area networks. He interfaces with all levels of user management to translate business network requirements to network system solutions. He reviews service-level requirements, equipment options, and costs with management. He analyzes and plans configurations based on this review, and coordinates the delivery of service, and interacts with external vendors as necessary.

Finding and Training Help Desk Personnel

In the past, information technology departments recruited help desk employees from technical staff. Now, however, these positions require a mix of technical skills, customer service talent, and willingness to learn. Help desk operators have been found among office personnel, teachers, customer service representatives, and recent computer science graduates. Skills required for the help desk include a knowledge of hardware and software, fast learning, patience, and a good telephone manner.

Most IT departments will also need to invest in aggressive training for support representatives, offering more in-depth education so that support personnel will be more knowledgeable than their clients. The stature of the help desk worker is being elevated as many are playing a more active role in choosing which software products get implemented. End users tend to go to highly paid professionals when a help desk cannot support a product. Training requirements are based upon the level of expertise needed for each individual help desk and the type of help desk software systems, tools, and techniques applied.

A training plan, including appropriate job descriptions, goals, expectations, and career paths, is developed based upon the unique needs of the help desk in question. Training encompasses both technical and nontechnical subject matter. An excellent means for developing a help desk training plan is to engage a consultant or outsourcer to help prepare it—from a detached perspective.

Help Wanted Ads for Help Desk Personnel

The following are from the Positions Available section of the Boston *Globe*™ and typically show what various help desks are seeking to staff their own support service.

Help Desk Specialist. Requirement: Analyze hardware, software and network problems, disruptions or outages. Communicate via telephone and E-mail to the users and It management. Understand the network software and be able to diagnose problems utilizing the network monitoring tools (NET-SYS, etc.). Understand the inner workings of "CICS." 1 to 3 years experience supporting a combination of the following software: Novell Network, MS DOS, Windows, Lotus 123, TSO, JCL, CICS, System 7, Excel, VTAM.

Senior Help Desk Analyst. This position provides technical support to clients, systems programmers and vendors to

Picture 13-1 Help desk training is a perpetual task

resolve problems incurred in the installation and ongoing operation of a wide range of data and voice communications products, on-line and operating systems to optimize machine performance and minimize downtime. you will lead and direct help desk projects and provide guidance and direction to less experienced staff. Qualified candidate must possess a Bachelor's degree of equivalent experience along with 3-5 years' related help desk experience. Requires thorough understanding of MVS-Host supervisor programs, data communication controllers, multiplexors, NETVIEW, CICS and TSO plus strong problem-solving analytical and communications skills.

Hotline Supervisor. This is an excellent opportunity for a service-oriented individual with hands-on experience managing a computer support-based hotline who is looking to join a progressive team in a supervisory capacity which will oversee our network support hotline, consisting of 290+ end-users operating a PC/Novell NetWare environment. This position has two primary functions. The first is to provide full-scope supervision of the network support hotline to include: staffing, training, scheduling, delegating and prioritizing of work assignments, and performance reviews for a staff of 3-5 specialists. The second function is to provide hands-on technical support and expertise to the immediate staff and end-user population, and to provide statistical reports, environmental analysis, and recommendations to management for improvement actions.

Qualified candidates should possess either a college degree in a computer-related field, or equivalent work experience with 2-4 years of experience supervising in a service/support environment. Proven analytical and problem-solving techniques, as well as strong interpersonal skills are required. You must be proficient with the hardware and software of IBM compatible PC's operating under both DOS and Windows, Novell NetWare, and various software applications.

Table 13-1 represents a sample quiz a potential employer might want to administer to a potential help desk specialist.

Table 13-1 Sample quiz for an aspiring help desk specialist

1. Why would you like to be a part of the help desk group, and how could you add value to the group?

2. What are the four SYSGEN Parameters that have impact on system crash and what do they do?

3. How can you identify a quorem disk on a cluster?

4. How many operating systems are you familiar with? Can you run errorlog/syserr?

5. Do you know the memory limits on 16, 18, 22 bit machines?

6. Do you consider yourself a generalist or specialist? Can you elaborate?

7. If a system is in a hung state, do you know how to force a crash to write out a dump file? (providing all necessary parameters are set up)?

8. What command would you use to identify firmware revision ports, requestors, devices, load, connections, etc.?

9. How do you boot from the console?

10. How is priority determined on a Q-bus?

11. When looking at communication port errors in the errorlog, how do you determine exactly what is causing the error?

12. A customer calls and states that his system is hung. How do you proceed?

13. You are experienced on tape drives and are sent to work on a new tape drive that you have never seen before. On site you are reading the tape tech manual when the customer comes in and begins to yell, "Haven't you been trained on this device?" How do you respond?

14. You are working in the CD group and have just completed a call. You phone the customer to inform them you have finished and the customer may now turn the key back to local, and you will notify your local office of your findings. The customer then asks, "What did you find?" How do you respond?

15. What is the difference between paging and swapping?

16. What are the general registers used for on boot?

17. What is the basic purpose of SYSGEN, AUTHORIZE, NCP, and MONITOR?

18. What do the terms LRP, SRP, and IRP indicate and how are they used?

Chapter

14

Ten Ideas for Re-engineering Your Help Desk

MICHAEL HAMMER AND JAMES CHAMPY, WHO CO-AU-
THORED *Re-engineering The Corporation—A Manifesto for Business Revolution*, define re-engineering as "the fundamental
rethinking and radical redesign of business processes to achieve
dramatic improvements in critical, contemporary measures of
performance, such as cost, quality, service, and speed." According to Hammer, processes involve all the work that gets
done between the start and finish, including, for example, the
processes between identifying a sales prospect to obtaining an
order, or, for service, the process between receiving an inquiry
and its resolution.

In that vein, then, we present ten ideas for re-engineering
the processes inherent in help desks:

1. *The best-of-the-best benchmark*. One of the ways to re-
engineer your help desk is to find out what the best one is,
within your industry or function, and emulate it, with some
improvements. This type of research is usually easy. In most

cases, help desk people like to show off their capabilities and often don't mind if the visitor is a competitor.

2. *Interactive TV.* Using interactive television or video conferencing as a medium to communicate opens the door to its use as a tool for diagnosis, analysis, synthesis, and, ultimately, a solution. The centralized resource could communicate with the customer, user, or field technician, eyeball to eyeball, in real time.

3. *Dispatcher diagnoses.* Most dispatchers, as a matter of common sense, train themselves to respond to certain patterns of symptoms. As they get more experienced and clever at it, they become better diagnosticians. This offloads the pressure to log some calls and makes customers and users happy because they don't have to wait for a secondary person to resolve the issue. The concept here is to formally train dispatchers to accept more technical responsibility or to employ "expert systems," referred to in Chapter 10.

4. *Roving call handlers.* Call handlers, especially technicians, could patrol certain areas in their vehicles, using cellular phones to keep in contact with home base—just like your friendly neighborhood policeman. This, like roving spare parts vans, increases the responsiveness to customers.

5. *Team call handlers.* Team call handlers tackle the problem, once and for all, at the outset of the call. They sit around the table with reference documents, desktop computers, fax machines, and telephones answering the customer, user, or service engineer problem on-line rather than having the call handed off serially.

6. *Management center.* The concept of the management center is explained in more detail in Section 3.

7. *Centralization.* As long as there are help desks, there will be a debate regarding centralizing the help desk functions into one "war room" or splitting them up according to geography, type of problem, type of product serviced, time zones, and so on. Looking purely at the nonlabor aspects of help desks, it seems that centralizing functions could be an effective re-engineering strategy.

8. *Outsourcing.* In certain situations, especially including a start-up, outsourcing the help desk would be a viable strategy for re-engineering a help desk. Outsourcing means giving the intellectual and physical responsibility for the help desk function to a specialist company that is not connected to the help desk corporation. Sometimes this involves transfers of the company's employees to the outsourcer.

9. *Fault/Fix library.* Developing and/or improving the help desk's fault/fix library will surely yield greater productivity. By constantly analyzing problems and classifying them, while matching them to appropriate solutions, the help desk learning curve will increase substantially.

10. *Artificial Intelligence.* Using artificial intelligence to anticipate and fix failures before they occur, without being evident to the customer, is a re-engineering strategy many help desks already employ. Some companies are seeking to automate help desks with "expert systems" that can prompt call handlers, technicians, or users through a series of questions to solve problems. Chapter 10 discusses artificial intelligence in more detail.

As companies start to focus on client server, interest in automated help desks increases dramatically. According to industry statistics, the strongest growing area of corporate automation is the help desk: almost 72 percent of survey respondents had automated the help desk to some degree or planned to do so. A year earlier, the survey found that only 18 percent of those surveyed had or planned to automate the help desk. Although may callers at first do not want to talk to a computer, they quickly change their minds if their problem is rapidly resolved using that method. You hardly ever talk to a human when you call a bank today, but you still get all your questions answered. End users want their needs met.

The Management Center Concept
A Virtual Help Desk

Chapter

15

Mini Management Centers

FOR THOSE OF US IN THE HELP DESK OR SERVICE MANAGE-MENT INDUSTRY, we tend to group all types of call centers into one major category, the help desk. There are differences among the major categories, but for the most part, there is more commonality than differences.

These examples of help desks have, or soon will, become mini management centers:

→ The service management call center

→ The systems management center

→ The user help desk

→ the telesales center

In this chapter we look at these four different help desks and discuss the tasks, issues, and even politics that have caused them to be differentiated from one another and the issues that keep them from being unified under a common management and direction. This analysis will be in the light of "pre–management center" theory.

Take a quick look at the vendors who provide these various help desks and you will find very few differences in their capabilities. One major difference is the marketing strategy and the targeted market for the product. The tools are much the same, although the screens and terminology are directed at specific audiences, such as sales/marketing, software specialists, the glass house and its large system management requirements, or field service management. Rarely is a product found that targets the enterprise and the CIO, CEO, CFO, etc. Although there is a high level of commonality in tasks and tools in these packages, there are some distinct features that differentiate these products. The following is a brief discussion of those features and the targeted needs they address.

The Service Management Call Center

The service management call center package is typically used by the maintenance organization. The product that is being maintained could be anything from computer systems and software to refrigerators and washing machines. The differentiating feature for this package is the disposition of field maintenance personnel and the logistics of the maintenance function.

The primary focus of this package is utilization of field engineers, product performance, and contractual commitments to customers in the field. While profitability and customer satisfaction are two conflicting objectives for the maintenance organization, the purpose of this package is to balance one against the other.

There is a heavy focus on contract management, product and personnel performance, management escalation, dispatch, and logistics. The tasks generally associated with this package are shown in Figure 15-1.

The Systems Management Center

While any of the functions that comprise the service management call center are common to the systems management center, the main mission of this type of help desk is the operation, management, and performance of computer systems.

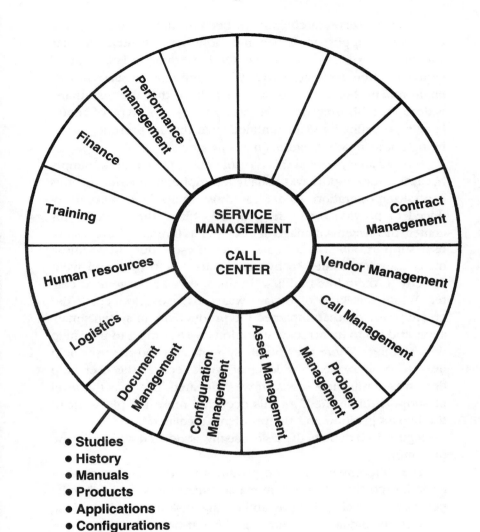

- Studies
- History
- Manuals
- Products
- Applications
- Configurations
- Archive

FIGURE 15-1 The service management call center: associated tasks

As client server architectures become more dominant and the system support tools become more sophisticated, the size and number of this type of center is declining. This type of center is often associated with the mainframe, or glass house, environment. Some would have us believe that the mainframe is dead, but this is far from the case. At most, this type of center is being redefined and streamlined such that its presence is not being felt as much it had been at one time.

We had always called this type of center a "help desk" simply because user support was usually a peripheral function for this centralized operation. As dedicated user help desks were introduced to provide better service and offload the work in this center, the systems management center still retained the task of user support, albeit at a higher level of escalation. In addition, many users continued to bypass the user help desk and went directly to their "ole buddies" in the systems management center. While this kind of bypass was usually overlooked, it did create problems that impacted the productivity of systems managers and led to incorrect assumptions with respect to user help desk staffing. Where the "buddy system" allowed the user help desk to be bypassed, the level of work seen at the user help desk was diminished, less staff was allocated, and thus the level of support diminished. As this occurred more people went to the bypass position and the problems escalated.

Figure 15-2 depicts the tasks usually associated with this type of center.

The differentiator for the products targeted at this type of desk lies mostly in the system management tools, which handle networks, capacity planning and tuning, disk management, logical security and access control, and batch processes. Operation of the system is the primary objective in this type of center, with user support and maintenance usually being outside its scope.

The User Help Desk

Initially, this type of desk was introduced to provide specialization in user support and to reduce the workload in the systems management center. Gradually, as more of the tasks

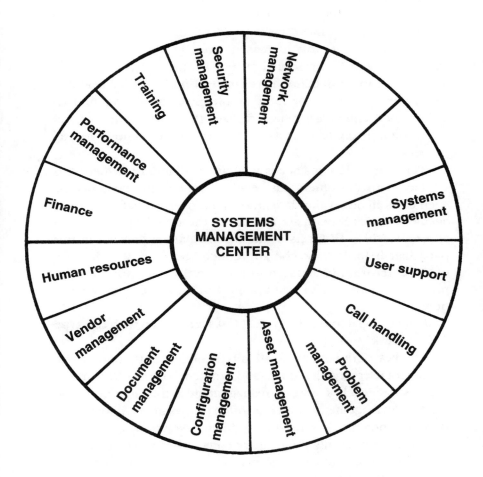

FIGURE 15-2 The systems management center: associated tasks

associated with the systems management center were automated, the user help desk took on more systems tasks, such as
access control. As more tasks were relegated to this type of
center, focus on its role increased. Even so, the view today of
this center and its personnel is that it might provide a quick
answer but in all likelihood will instead find another resource
to answer a question or fix a problem. Rarely do we find an
enlightened enterprise which realizes that this center is quite
often the only contact for its customers, not to mention its employees.

There are a few instances we have encountered where this
contact with customers has received much attention. In one
such case, all newly hired, degreed, employees targeted for management careers spend six months in the user help desk as an
apprenticeship. All facets of the business are supported in this
particular help desk, so the apprentices get a fairly wide view
of the enterprise. In addition to learning the enterprise, the ap-
prentice is exposed to technology and customer communications.

Figure 15-3 depicts the typical tasks associated with this type
of help desk.

The key differentiator for this type of center is communications with users, call handling, and problem solving. While there
is still some level of systems management at this help desk, the
systems management center is often the primary contact for
system problems. For on-site problem resolution, the service
organization is usually the primary contact for management and
dispatch of the problem. The main emphasis for the user help
desk is on user satisfaction, call closure, and problem solving.

The Telesales Center

While this type of center does not seem to be in the same
category as the previous three, there is a common thread that
classifies it as a help desk of a sort. The tools, communications,
and client contact are all common elements.

Generally, the creation of a telesales center is initiated in the
sale function of an enterprise, not in the technical functions of

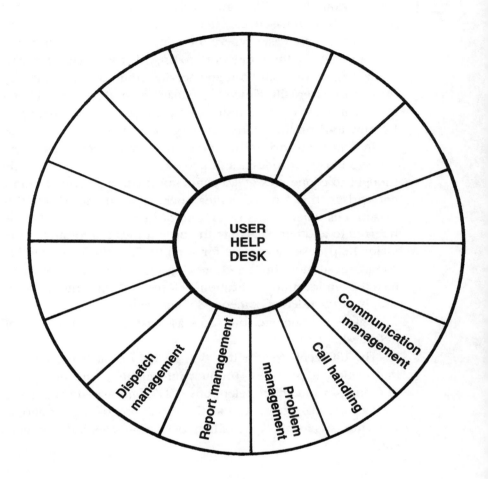

FIGURE 15-3 User Help Desk

the previous three. Planning, design, installation, and training are usually purchased externally as a complete package, although there are cases where the sales function has contracted any of the above three functions to provide the service. Systems management, user support, and service could be contracted internally or externally. However, management of the overall operation is usually retained in the sales organization, and sharing of information and tools rarely goes beyond the sales boundaries.

In larger enterprises, there tend to be many of these centers across industry, product, and geographic lines with very little thought to economies of scale and information sharing. In most enterprises, this type of center operates as an island; for this reason, customers often reach one of these centers only to be referred to another. Reaching the proper location for any of the major help desk categories for a particular enterprise has become a customer "hunt and peck" game where calls are transferred from location to location, referred to other numbers, or simply dead-ended at someone's voice mail.

Figure 15-4 depicts the tasks associated with this type of help desk.

The differentiator for this type of help desk is the type of information it provides (product information), the heavy use of computer integrated telephony (CIT), automated dialing and contact list management, and the order processing functions. The emphasis for this type of help desk is on sales and sales generation.

15-4 Telesales/Sales Center

Chapter

16

The Management Center

*I*N DEVELOPING OUR CONCEPT OF THE MANAGEMENT CENTER, we will look at many of the tools for various disciplines existing today in the help desk domain. We will explore tools not traditionally part of the help desk, tools already integrated by help desk software vendors, and some tools that may not even yet exist.

The real purpose of this chapter is to set something of a direction for our profession. Any success in developing something even close to the *ideal* management center is dependent on a global dialogue on the subject. Acceptance of a concept such as this starts out with a very basic problem and passes through many more complex problems.

The successful management center of the future must incorporate such things as currency conversion as a standard offering, global networks, on-line import/export tools, national and transnational shipping, duties, exceptions, etc.—and we have not even discussed the problems with languages other than English. Generally, English is the international business *"lingua franca,"* but in the help desk area, the audience is much wider than that of the general business world. Thus the need to address the language issue must be raised in our discussion of the management center.

In chapter 15 we discussed the different types of help desks. In this chapter we will try to pull them all together in an enterprise level view. Table 16-1 details the different tasks associated with each type of help desk. The intent is to highlight the commonality of tasks so that there is a better understanding of the redundancies that exist in the multiple help desks in our industry today.

Many of the tasks in Table 16-1 could be moved around to become part of another function, or many could reside within multiple functions. The point is that the tasks are very redundant, requiring much the same software tools and expertise to manage them.

Table 16-1 depicts a somewhat consolidated view of functions and tasks viewed at the enterprise level. We will pull one piece of our view and begin filling in the pieces one by one, starting with asset management only because there needs to be a starting point.

Asset Management

Our starting point in this world is the wonderful world of asset management (Figure 16-1). Although one of the simplest of our disciplines, with the most impact on the bottom line, it is the least practiced and most ignored of all the disciplines. One of the reasons for this is the fact that most enterprises already have assets that were accumulated over time; the need for asset management is not usually foreseen in the early stages of an enterprise. As the enterprise grows and realization kicks in with respect to the value of assets, it is most often too late to get control. The task of putting order into chaos appears overwhelming. However, while appearing to be terribly complex, it is not!

The greatest hurdle to overcome is the fact that since real control of an enterprise's assets has been ignored for so long, the corporate ledgers are out of whack. While this may be one of the simplest tasks faced by a service or help desk professional, it remains the most elusive of all corporate controls and management functions. The problem really has been political, like most

Table 16-1 Call Center Functions

Task	Service Management Call Center	Systems Management Center	User Help Desk	Telesales Center
Asset Management	X	X	X	X
Warranty	X		X	
Depreciation	X	X		
Configuratio Management	X	X	X	
Engineering Changes	X	X	X	
Moves/Adds and Changes	X	X	X	
License Management				
Testing, Staging	X			
Revision Control	X		X	
Documentation Management	X	X	X	X
Configuration Maps	X	X	X	
Drawings	X	X		
Specifications	X	X		
Logistics	X		X	
Duties, Customs Taxes and Tariffs	X			
Installation	X			
Shipping	X			X
Network Management	X			
Data	X	X		
Voice		X		
Facilities Management	X	X		
HVAC	X	X		
Cable Plant	X	X		
Performance Management	X	X		
Performance Monitoring		X	X	
Performance Engineering		X		
Performance Analysis	X	X	X	

Table 16-1 Call Center Functions (continued)

Task	Service Management Call Center	Systems Management Center	User Help Desk	Telesales Center
Human Resources	X	X	X	X
Training	X	X	X	X
Life Cycle Costing		X		
Transaction Based Costing	X		X	
Activity Based Costing	X	X	X	X
Accounts Payable Receivable	X			X
Risk Management	X	X		
Security Management		X	X	
Sales Management	X			X
Service Management	X			
Spares Kit	X			
Depot Repair	X			
Tooling	X			
User Support	X	X	X	
Systems Management		X	X	
System Tuning		X		
Capacity Planning		X		
Disk/Tape Management		X		
Change Management	X	X	X	
Call Handling	X	X	X	X
Problem Management	X	X	X	
Dispatch	X		X	
On-site	X			
Fault Analysis	X	X	X	
Remote Analysis	X		X	
Quality Control Messaging	X	X	X	X

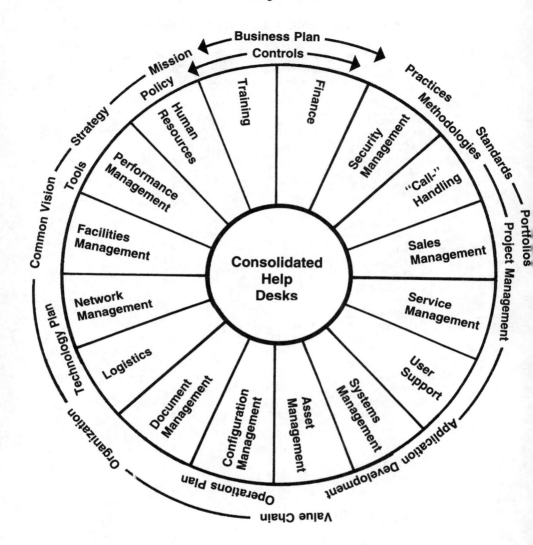

Figure 16-1   Management center—consolidated help desks

other problems we will encounter in the management center, but it also presents a significant financial problem—the book value of the enterprise itself.

There are many products available today that will capture and manage assets. As service and help desk professionals, we are all familiar with asset management packages that are integrated into service or help desk management software packages (HD packages). There are, of course, some high-cost, stand-alone monsters on the market, but asset management modules in most of today's HD packages are more than adequate for the average asset management needs, and many are adequate for the enterprise level management of assets.

Probably the best place to start is with the definition of asset management. Asset management means different things to different folks. Several definitions follow.

Domain Assets

Those assets in excess of $1,000 are usually under the control of a midlevel manager. These can be:

- Workstations, up to the board or license level

- Desks, furniture, decorations, etc.

- Tools and software

- Software licenses

Divisional Assets

Here we are concerned with a consolidated report of those domain assets that come under a divisional or first-level manager, the aggregate value of which could be significant, depending on the size of the enterprise. These divisional assets can be:

- Workstations

- Systems

- Vehicles

- Phone systems

- Capital equipment of any nature

Regional Assets

These assets can be significant in much the same way the divisional assets are. Depending on the way the enterprise is organized, either the region or the division may be the larger. Regional assets are usually significant in the enterprise sense. These are usually:

- Capital equipment

- Communications telephone vs. data

- Transportation

- Local Area Network costs

Area Assets

Area assets usually comprise some collection of regional, divisional, and domain assets. Their value is increasing as the view to smaller pieces is being reduced and the asset problem in the enterprise is becoming more of a global or international concern. Area assets include:

→ Consolidating capital equipment

→ Wide Area Network costs

→ Transportation

→ Communications

→ Facilities

→ Corporate S/W licenses

Global Assets

This is a fairly large view of the asset problem. Very few companies have a handle on this area of assets. This is usually the killing ground for audit firms. No audit firm has been able to investigate this area to the extent that should be required under any national laws. Due to the complexity of politics, purview, power struggles, and many other non-business related issues, control is lost and abuse is rampant.

The global asset is usually the same as the enterprise asset, but it is collected in a different fashion and delayed by geography and custom. Collection and consolidation of the enterprise asset is encumbered by anywhere from three to four area managers, divided in any number of ways, but usually geographic. Geographic splits can be either three-way (includes the Americas [North and South], the Pacific Rim [Asia, Japan, and ANZAC], and Europe and Africa) or four-way (includes the Americas, Europe, Africa, and Australia). Perhaps one day some enlightened enterprise will come along and divide its corporate structure in a fashion that more closely fits global sensitivities such as industry, religion, culture, nationality, and the individual customer.

Enterprise Assets

This is the area of focus for us. We have always seen the simplicity and importance, the abuses and the excuses, the waste and the fraud. The Enterprise Asset is the most elusive. No one has been able to bring this under control simply because politics, accounting practices, and cross-functional communication problems will not allow for it to happen.

Enterprise assets are those which show up in the annual report to reflect the value of the company in terms of things that are tangible and convertible to real dollars. No one has been able to define these assets. Auditing firms worldwide vary on the subject, but for the most part, the enterprise-level managers define this area to suit their own interests. There is, however, one constant in the success of a company—Wall Street. Assets set the value of a company; if a company fails we can still retrieve our investment by selling off assets. Of course, this means we trust the enterprise managers to accurately assess the value of the assets (which is generally not the case).

When dealing at the enterprise level of asset management we become involved with such things as buildings, land, people, capital equipment, and expendables. We need to define what we will record as an asset. All too few companies have actually defined the level at which they record assets. Since this is much the purview of the tax authorities, the authors make no specific recommendations. However, since we have not yet shied away from making statements, here is our guide for viewing assets, from the smallest (#1) to the largest (#6).

1. **Component level.**

2. **Workstation/PC/Laptop.**

3. **Systems**

4. **Buildings and facilities**

5. **People** (including cost, investment in training, and experience)

6. **Transportation** (vehicles, aircraft, etc.)

An enterprise needs to make some decisions about the style of management it will employ. If the enterprise is solely concerned with the value of its stock, then assets will be valued at the highest possible value. In most cases the enterprise will have no real need for assets management since it will only value its assets at that point which is needed to keep the company stock as highly valued as possible. Companies of this type include both bluechips and "fly-by-nights." Inflating enterprise value is a Wall Street custom.

There will be a difference between what you think the actual asset value of a given enterprise is and value the enterprise must reflect to an investor in your company. Both authors worked for corporations that inflated their assets significantly. The original source of the inflation was not a desire to deceive but rather ignorance of the real value of the corporation. As time went on and there was more understanding of the corporation's actual value, it became too late to correct it without a drastic one-time write-off charge to the books. To most of the major corporations, this write-off charge would mean the difference between showing a profit or loss in that year, or significant investor impact via stock value.

Why do we tell you this? Because the problem is not just technical or disciplinary. It is more than an insular help desk or service management professional can see. Only the professional with a global view could begin to understand it. As professionals we are responsible for looking in all directions to understand all levels of asset management, be they crossfunctional, domain, divisional, regional, area, global, or enterprise.

There are certain basic factors your enterprise will need to address in order to achieve enterprise level control.

Definition of assets. Are desks to be included as an asset? Chairs? PC components? Laptops? Buildings? HVAC?

Support. Your enterprise will need both cross-functional and geographic support in order to achieve control.

Time. Depending on the perceived discrepancies between the actual and stated values of your enterprise, the financial assessment process may need to be budgeted over a period of years to minimize the financial impact. Working with treasury/ finance is a must.

A plan. Achieving control requires an attack plan which specifies locations, products, facilities, personnel, etc.

Personnel. Utilization of the "tiger team" approach is extremely effective in achieving consistency. Depending on the size of the enterprise, these teams would be in place for a number of years. The type of personnel and the fixed length of this kind of project would indicate the use of an outsourcer or fixed-length contract employees.

Policy and procedural documents. To achieve enterprise control, working with personnel/human resources is essential. Failure to document and enforce punitive measures dooms this effort to failure. The old saw that punitive policies are "not a corporate custom" is drivel. Policies must protect the enterprise from abuse. The idea that policies against theft and fraud should not be published and enforced simply invites disaster. If a laptop is signed out to an employee and that employee no longer has it, there's a problem. If the employee leaves and the laptop somehow leaves with the employee, there is a problem. In both instances there must be penalties for abuse, including the civil court.

Control of new assets. The attack plan must include the coincident control of new assets. Focus on a domain by domain level plan must not preclude the adoption of controls for new assets coming in at the enterprise level.

Help desk or service management packages. With a view to our yet-to-be-created management center, the packages should be capable at this point of at least being able to handle the defined requirements of the enterprise asset. They should not only be capable of asset management but they should also be able to integrate these assets into the configuration management module or discipline. As assets move, are added, or are changed, the configuration management module should reflect the change.

Automated tagging and bar coding. During the process of collecting our data, we should have an integrated set of products that allow for bar coding. The first time through, the collection process will be long and tedious. However, by utilizing the proper tools such as wireless, hand-held terminals capable of printing bar code labels, interfaced with the help desk or service management system, the task becomes much easier. Future floor-to-book-asset takes are a simple matter of "shooting" the bar code with the same handheld terminal and a bar code wand.

Configuration Management

Looking at our management center pie again, we will now add in the configuration management piece.

As we attain some level of control of our assets, untagged and new, we need to know where they are and where they fit in the enterprise. Configuration management is usually provided with most of today's help desk and service management packages as either a standard module or an option. However, to us, configuration management is not an option. Whether in a small or a large enterprise, strict adherence to asset and configuration management principles is a must. Tasks include:

→ *Connections*—This includes all remote, in-house, carrier, and utility communications required to connect the enterprise from the domain on up. It should also include diagrams for the "cable plant" or facility wiring. Products available today provide graphic presentations of the Wide and Local Area Networks to enhance troubleshooting and reduce downtime. Technology is rapidly automating many of the tasks that once required network specialists.

→ *Revision history*—As changes are made to any assets, the configuration must be updated either manually or automatically. Most of today's packages have automated this function. Generally, revisions cover changes to components in the system. Any new software versions introduced to the system can be impacted by out-of-date components. Any component swapped in the repair process must also be reflected in the configuration.

→ *Modifications*—These also have a major impact on the configuration, whether hardware or software. This function becomes all that much more important if the enterprise is developing its own applications. Poor control will inevitably cause major problems.

→ *Moves/Adds/Changes*—This is also a task of the configuration management function. With personnel shifts, attrition, transfers, etc., it is an important enterprise control. Its automation should include the updating of the asset management function.

→ *Licensing*—While the control of software licensing might easily be part of configuration management, we cover this task under the contract management function.

Configuration management, like asset management, is extremely difficult to control, especially if it has been ignored in the past. Getting it under control and keeping it under control requires a concerted effort. It also has political pitfalls that the help desk or service management professional should be aware of.

Today the configuration management function is disseminated throughout the enterprise. Some of the different factions in the enterprise that have a piece of this responsibility are the system manager (after all, it's part of the enterprise system); the network manager (what do system managers know about telephony?); the area or country MIS manager (what do the corporate managers know about local carriers and legalities?); and the CIO (what do any of the above know, they'll just do as I say!).

If any of the above looks familiar, you will understand the formidable road ahead to the Management Center, but for the moment: on to Network Management.

Network Management

The network management function comprises a number of tasks. They include:

• Management and control of the network configuration, from local to wide area;

• Maintaining the configuration, including product, connectivity, and service providers;

• Providing access control for users;

• Providing documentation and maps of the network, including changes, moves, adds, problems, etc.;

• Maintaining the configuration and security;

• Managing network alarms and faults to resolution; and

• Maintaining the wide area to local area history of moves, adds, changes, architecture, and problems.

Most help desk packages today will include an interface to one of the many network management packages. As more of the various tasks in network management become automated, there will be less reliance on the network specialists. However, today the need for network specialists is essential for almost any size network. All types of help desks, even systems management centers, tend to partition the network management role into a separate function.

There is a trend to outsource this function, based on its degree of difficulty, to larger communication providers who are expanding their services to network outsourcing. This is difficult to manage at the enterprise level because network service providers are usually regulated by law, which varies from country to country. Most enterprises are ill prepared to take on this global task. To complicate the issue, debate over architectures, standards, and practices not only rage from country to country and vendor to vendor but also even within the enterprise. It appears that this situation will continue to exist for the short term until the demand to automate or standarize these tasks is met. This demand is already peaking as groupware products, remote access and downloads, and shared databases are implemented and network problems get more visibility at the senior levels of enterprise.

The management center view of network management requires tight integration with the configuration and asset management functions. Network management products are capable of identifying types of modems, servers, users, revisions, etc. Data captured by the network management product should be shared with all other functions in the management center and vice versa. Today, very little progress has been made to reduce the redundancies in these products.

Document Management

The document management function defines the scope and handling of all forms of documentation with respect to information systems. Its definition is being expanded to include the management and sharing of information throughout the enterprise. As one of the functions within the management center, the introduction of shared databases, internet access and homepages, and archival needs is getting much more attention in service management and help desk Packages.

Some of the types of material included in this function are:

— Technical manuals

— Archives—not only those applicable to the information systems, but also those business documents the enterprise is legally bound to retain

— Engineering changes and revisions

— Publications

— Personnel records

— User manuals

— Product/Portfolio brochures

— Industry studies

— Application development code and changes

— Product development documents

— Customer profiles

— Configuration documents

Document management is a need that applies to the entire organization. One of the first steps in applying this function properly is to define what the particular enterprise means by documents—what documents must be retained by law, for continuity of the enterprise or entities within the enterprise, and, in fact, what is meant by the term document.

With more enterprises opening up homepages on the Internet, sharing information with external organizations, and moving to distributed databases, it becomes more critical every day to ensure that documentation within the enterprise is properly distributed, shared, accessible, and protected. Many documents could appropriately be classified as an asset, giving significant value to the knowledge contained therein.

Document management needs to be firmly embedded in an enterprise's methodology, and adherence to controls should be regulated by firm policy. As enterprises continue to downsize, the outflow of the enterprise's intellectual property is a massive problem.

Security Management

There are two major categories of security management: logical and physical. *Logical security* is concerned with the security of information technology. It includes access control; gateways to protect infiltration via services such as Internet or other on-line services; proper focus on physical security so that system security is not breached by physical access; and monitoring of user activity to identify unusual trends, breaches of security, or unauthorized use of user services. *Physical Security* is usually more concerned with access to facilities and controlled spaces within facilities. It includes physical access; identification badges and control; and parking lot lighting and monitoring for safety.

Typically the two types of security are handled by separate organizations within the enterprise. Physical security tends to be either handled by the facilities personnel or outsourced to companies specializing in physical security management. Logical security is usually relegated to the systems management function.

However, there are many untried opportunities to integrate the two functions. Starting with the outsourcing of physical security, no one can expect the "rent a cop" to fully understand what or whom to watch for in accessing a facility. Neither can he be expected to understand the basic value of intellectual material that may be lost. When a laptop computer can be placed in a briefcase and thus leave a facility, the enterprise is facing a massive problem, not only in loss of intellectual material but in assets as well.

Should any enterprise wish to impose effective security policies, it would be required to fully document the policies, define assets and intellectual property, and, on top of that, clearly define punitive actions for termination. While termination of employees will help, the enterprise must also define the legal actions it will take for certain breaches of security. Most enterprises shy away from both types of actions as being "drastic" or harsh. However, employees know right from wrong and would see this type of policy and procedure a necessary practice. Any employee who shows anger at the imposition of such practices bears watching in our point of view.

Systems Management

The systems management function is also being redefined in the enterprise today. As more tasks associated with the management of systems become automated or outsourced, the "MIS" department needs to be re-engineered. As more tasks become embedded in the software tools, the number of personnel that has historically been needed to manage larger operations is dwindling.

For the established MIS department, the necessity to downsize has been slow in happening. Rather than face facts, many of these organizations have taken an alternate route to downsizing; they have created their own little enterprises within, specializing in consulting or outsourcing. Selling excess resources and capacity, while delaying the inevitable usually ends as a downsizing exercise eventually. Only larger enterprises can be successful at entering the "outsourcing" business. The problem will always remain, however, that the outsourcing department is not considered "core" by the enterprise itself.

Systems managers will continue to be needed, but the number of staff will diminish. With the increased number of enterprises going to distributed architectures, users themselves will become virtual systems managers. Even in a "Lights Out" or unattended operation, there still remains a need for someone to turn out the lights. Some of the tasks have already been incorporated in many of the help desk packages to the point that the systems manager today could actually be the person at the help desk. These tasks include:

▶ Console management

▶ Remote management

▶ Access control

▶ Logical security

▶ Batch/network/system alarm automation and intervention

▶ Capacity planning

Human Resources Management

Generally speaking, the HR function is separate from most other functions within the enterprise. The rationale is that the information on personnel is so sensitive that it needs to be isolated from the mainstream. However, databases on personnel, location, badge numbers, identification, management level, et al., are kept in detail by service management and help desk packages.

Separating the functions results in massive redundancies, and the argument that personnel databases should be kept isolated to ensure confidentiality does not fly anymore. What could be more sensitive than managing a user's access, passwords, and even access to user files? The management center needs to integrate all the functions of human resources. In doing so, access to skills and resources that exist within the enterprise is more accessible, and productivity gains would result. Most help desk and service management packages already have multi-level security capabilities such that employee benefits, compensation, et al., can be protected while providing a lower level of security to enable access to simple employee directories and locators.

Vendor Management

Critical to the enterprise is the control of purchasing, partnering, and provision of services. Most of today's help desk and service management packages document the vendors, their responsibilities, scope of work, contractual commitments, and deployment. Much of the relationship is already automated via E-mail or even by providing the vendors with access to the help desk or service management system.

In the management center, the vendor plays a proper role in managing its own commitments, with the system monitoring performance. Intervention by enterprise staff is taken only when anomalies, which are noted by the system itself, occur. Variances in response time, repair time, or downtime are all noted by any good service package and are compared with the established, contracted parameters by which the vendor must perform. Penalty clauses are automatically implemented with little intervention required by staff.

"Vendor" includes the providers of not only information technology but also stationery, supplies, office equipment, HVAC, fleet cars, etc. For effective vendor management, the enterprise must have a clearly defined, published, value chain, which achieves the best cost and product. This value chain must include the supply of products and services to the enterprise and the enterprise customers as well. Any good "value chain" methodology avoids conflicts with customers who are vendors as well. For instance, if one of your customers is Ford Motors, your purchasing department should not purchase a fleet of vehicles from Toyota.

Service Management

This function is concerned with deployment of service technicians to repair and maintain the internal or external product. Service management packages today include automated dispatch, problem tracking, fault isolation, predictive sparing and kits for deployment, call history, contractual commitments, etc. Most of the functions we have already discussed are part of service management packages today. Training is also a critical piece of this function, although it is treated as a separate function in the management center.

Service management tasks include:

√**Problem management**	√**Contract base**
√**Performance measurements**	√**Cost analysis**
√**Trend analysis**	√**Productivity levels**
√**Supply and support**	√**Warranty control**
√**Logistics and deployment**	√**Accounts payable/receivable**
√**Administration**	√**Contract renewal**

Call Handling

While considered part of the service management function, call handling is also part of the help desk and telesales functions. Problem calls must be routed to different areas for resolution, but someone needs to own responsibility for ensuring closure. This is usually the first contact on the call. In additon, this function, if properly implemented, includes an effective automated call director and automated dissemination of solutions for customer queries.

One of the keys to successful call management is the actual analysis, forecasting, and planning for call staff. Call queuing theory provides a set of tables, in use by telephone companies for years, to develop a plan for appropriate levels of staff. For the most part, our industry today makes a best guess based on available statistics and averages for numbers of calls, time to close, and other algorithms; for the most part, this staffing is not yet a science.

As we approach the management center, the centralized concentration of help desk and service management call staff will also change its profile. With new switching products and improved communications and bandwidth, the day will come when this kind of staff works out of the home office. We may even see a reincarnation of the Industrial Age concept of "piece work." Work-at-home call staff could work when and for as long as they prefer and would be paid on a "per call" basis.

Also essential for the successful call center are the knowledge systems for problem resolution. There are many types available today, such as AI based learning engines, hypertext search, knowledge trees, etc. For problem resolution these are essential, but, due to their basic design, their applicability could be taken beyond the information technology environment into the enterprise itself. All that needs to be done to accomplish this jump is to redefine the term *problem*.

Problem currently means IT outages, failures, loss of communications, bugs, etc., but problem should be redefined to include policy application, location of management for emergency, and management procedures for issues. At that point, the management center would begin to take on more of a global role in the enterprise.

Performance Management

Many of today's service management and help desk packages include the capability of monitoring the performance of the system. Much of the criteria is focused on predictive failure analysis, but more often we are seeing the use of benchmarks and parameters to measure a systems performance against a baseline. Baselines can be anything from the vendor specification to enterprise expectation. Failure to meet the established criteria results in some action by a subfunction called performance engineering. This function could be internal engineering or vendor engineering. Performance management is still barely practiced in the enterprise even though its principles could be applied beyond technology to the performance of the enterprise and its employees.

The tasks within this function are:

☐ Performance criteria design

☐ Performance monitoring

☐ Performance engineering

☐ Performance change requests and cost analysis

Having described some of the functions that would be included in a management center, it is now necessary to describe the glue that would hold it all together. It should be the goal of all entities within an enterprise, after assessing all the enterprise's functions and identifying the economies of a real management center, to tie the enterprise together and diminish its many little islands of functions and tasks.

Business Planning

Business planning is not an easy task and is probably best performed by an external consultant: Trying to do your own is much like taking out your own appendix. The business plan must be tied together at the enterprise level and should define the business, organization, and strategies. It should address not only the business considerations but also the geographical, cultural, technological, and organizational needs for moving to a decentralized operation based on a centralized database.

Operations Planning

Moving from the business plan, the operations plan must take the enterprise to a higher level of detail, specifying which functions will be implemented, the definitions of such things as assets, and policies and procedures to be applied. Again, this plan must take into account the management center capability. Since most business planning is done at the level of senior managers and resides in the realm of the management sciences, it cannot be expected that senior managers would understand the capabilities, issues, resources, and economies that could be achieved. Teams that pair the management scientist with the management technologist would be able to develop such a plan.

Technology Plan

Another piece of the enterprise glue is the technology plan. This plan could be a massive document defining each and every application within the enterprise. But it could also be as simple as stating that all IT acquisition will be purchased off the shelf and will adhere to specific standards and conventions. The key to the technoloy plan is ensuring common information and communication structure to manage the global enterprise.

Methodology

Methodology is another key element in the glue that holds the enterprise together. Today, most enterprises have multiple methodologies for such functions as software development, customer service, management, or tools. Various disciplines represented here may have unique requirements for their own methodologies, but they cannot continue to be isolated from one another if an enterprise is to shift to a true management center. The addition of an enterprise methodology that can consolidate the various methodologies at a higher level to ensure consistency, continuity, and communication across each of them is essential.

Failure to employ existing methodologies is another big problem. There are very few enterprises that audit the application and documentation of a particular methodology. Without punitive policies in place to ensure adherence, the enterprise might just as well not spend the time or money on a methodology.

Evaluating and Implementing Help Desk Software

Chapter

17

The Essentials of Help Desk Software—How to Pick a Winner

Obligation Management Packages

*T*HE OBLIGATION MANAGEMENT SYSTEM IS THE **financial** heart of a service management system. It manages and maintains the integrity of customer service contracts and other relationships, including warranty details or "time and materials" conditions. The full life cycle of the business relationship is managed with a minimum of administrative effort. Starting with the initial quotation and following the process through acceptance, changes to contract terms or items, repricing, renewal, and termination, the system maximizes automation and accuracy without sacrificing financial control or flexibility.

By meeting clients' precise needs, the highest levels of customer satisfaction and profit can be achieved. However, good service management requires that service contracts be flexible enough to contain all the different types and levels of service any client might desire. This frees the service organization from the impossible constraints that would exist if they were trying to manage such a flexible and customer-driven marketing policy by normal methods. An advanced pricing mechanism allows a vast range of different contracts to be charged in proportion to their expected costs.

Obligation management facilitates effective control of invoices and periodic earnings. Any changes are reflected in future invoices and earnings on a daily pro rata basis and generate, where necessary, immediate invoices to address any overlooked revenues. "What if" facilities show detailed financial analyses and provide cash flow forecasts, periodic income, and sales reserve balances by customer, contract, site, product, or areas.

Service Profitability

Most service organizations suffer from a lack of truly accurate information about which parts of their operations are profitable and which are not. Integrated systems accumulate costs and revenues from the entire business to provide an accurate and up-to-date view of profitability by customer, contract, site, product, or self-managed business unit. Consequently, managers can make thoroughly informed and accurate decisions about how to price future service offerings and address those contracts that are consistently costing more than they generate in revenue.

Call Handling Packages

To cope with the increasing demand for service, help desk operations are using software products that log and track calls and assist in expediting answers to a variety of questions. Expert systems technology is being incorporated into, or used in conjunction with, many help desk products. These are multifaceted systems that use a set of rules to help determine answers to problems. Case-based reasoning (in which prior cases are used to provide answers) and multimedia are being incorporated into many products in order to visualize a piece of equipment and guide the user through a series of operations. A number of software packages allow the user to dial in and access the diagnosis-and-solving portion of their products. This substantially reduces the number of calls fielded by help desk personnel, but yet provides timely and quality service to the end user.

Although most software packages require a dedicated host, client/server versions of help desk applications are becoming increasingly popular. Users want help desk packages that can be integrated with existing electronic mail systems and network management programs. The help desk programs now available are able to run on only a few operating systems, but the number of platforms is expected to expand. Many help desk software publishers are incorporating expert system functionality into their products to solve more problems expediently. This help desk software assists in four main areas:

1. Operators create and complete service call records on line, so that information of a historical nature is readily available.

2. Information is maintained regarding the current availability, capabilities, and location of field service engineers.

3. Problem calls and outstanding calls are continually highlighted so that contractual obligations can be met.

4. Comprehensive site and equipment information is made available and changes of location are dynamically updated by the operators.

The help desk package should be interactive. Operators are prompted to carry out necessary transactions in a logical manner while dealing with incoming calls. Search facilities should allow the operator to find information quickly from any of the following prompts: customer name, contract number, serial number, site telephone number, and site mail stop.

As the problem symptom is recorded, records of customer purchase order numbers are created, and any likelihood of warranty or suspected recall can be shown. The date and time of the incoming call is automatically logged by the system. At the same time, a unique job number is assigned to create a permanent audit trail. A hard copy printout is provided to ensure that documented evidence exists as a backup in the event of machine failure. A call can be left unassigned or, alternatively, a servicer can be selected immediately. Any scheduled arrival date or time given to the customer is recorded on the system.

Help desk software holds information regarding product training and skill levels of servicers, permitting the most suitable one to be selected for a certain task. It reports upon the financial status of the customer, the scope of the contract coverage, response deadlines, and whether the contract has been paid or is still unpaid. Details of the last site visit and further useful information (such as special instructions, facilities or hours or permitted access) are also shown. The system can advise of any other calls that may be open at the same site to permit more effective use of labor. Similarly, it can also advise of other outstanding calls on the same time, thus preventing duplicated callout if another member of the customer's staff has reported the fault, or parts are awaiting installation.

While paperwork relating to completed service calls may be batch input to the system at a later stage, help desk software also offers a two-stage call for completion procedure. During the first stage, the system is continually updated in real time immediately after calls are finished. Partial completion with details of service time and parts used, outstanding, or exchanged are recorded to keep accurate records of parts at any specific location at all times. This triggers a purchase order processing system, which starts procurement at the primary or remote parts storage locations if parts have fallen below the minimum recommended levels.

Final details of time recording, work completed, traveling, and miscellaneous expenses can be completed in a batch mode at the second stage on receipt of the signed paperwork. This second stage prepares invoicing for time and materials and non-contract work. Maintenance arising from causes such as customer negligence can also be detected and reported for management review. After completing the first stage, the operator can move quickly to select and read the next call allocated to the servicer. When this is dispatched over the telephone, the system updates the new location of the servicer and his parts stock.

Procedures Following Completion of a Call

After the calls are completed, three invoice types can be created. The first relates to calls on a time-and-material basis, where the contract might cover repairs, but not traveling time or costs. The second type is where the work carried out is completely covered under the contract and not chargeable to the customer. The third type of invoice is where some doubt about coverage exists (such as work required as a result of user negligence or warranty).

The system maintains records about parts used, non-stock parts used, exchanges of parts in and out, and parts outstanding. It forces entry of serial numbers of parts to be made where applicable, thus creating a traceable audit trail for those items. It automatically opens calls for future visits when spare parts are unavailable or if there is a need to allocate more than one servicer to the task.

There should be no practical limit to the number of contracts, customers, or servicers that can be handled by help desk software. Furthermore, a group user should be able to independently record the transactions of many companies, including their many branches or regions, on the same system.

Scheduling Servicers

A record for each servicer can be automatically kept by the help desk system. Thus, any manager or call handler anywhere on the system can view a particular servicer's outstanding calls, allocated calls, calls completed but awaiting the return of paperwork, and his current whereabouts. Future absences for training courses, holidays, or even brief personal absences are recorded by the system. This is particularly useful where an operator wishes to schedule work such as preventative maintenance visits. Both features assist managers in matching future workloads against available resources.

The call record also shows call log numbers, date and time received, reported fault, product type, customer name, address, and the call's priority for any date or period requested. The progress of any particular job is automatically monitored by "tickler" procedures, which will indicate that an excessive amount of time is being taken to complete the visit. The site location telephone number is displayed, allowing the operator to obtain up-to-the-minute information from the servicer and to reassess the situation if required.

The servicer's location screen shows the location of any, or all, servicers. The call log number, name of customer, problem symptom, and zip code are displayed together with the servicer's date and time of dispatch to that site. Another option shows servicer availability by product type and skill level. A list can then be displayed of all suitably qualified available servicers and their workload. Unavailable servicers are listed with reasons for their temporary absence.

Open Calls

All outstanding calls can be listed to show both unallocated calls and those allocated to a particular servicer. The system displays the log number of the call, site zip code, description of the item, and the fault reported. Allocation or reallocation of calls from this list can also be carried out and the rest of the system updated. The outstanding call system tracks the progress of all calls and takes into account the contractually agreed response time, elapsed time since the call was logged, and escalation priorities.

An escalation program displays the number of calls that have gone into the escalation status at the top of designated terminal screens. The system can be interrogated at any time to show the detail of calls in this status. The calls are listed in order with the "worst" one at the top. All this "emergency" or status information can also be displayed on a single screen by using color codes instead of separate screens.

Spare Parts Finder

The parts finder option gives the call handling operator the ability to identify and locate part numbers and the location of any parts or supplies that may be required to fulfill an incoming call. This is extremely useful before allocating a service engineer.

Because the parts control system also tracks quantities of available matériel, it can lead to more productive uses of manpower by determining if a part is available before assigning a call.

Call Review

The call status feature allows financial managers and service managers to review current calls selectively by a range of log numbers or servicers. It allows real time investigation of the number of calls received on a certain day, as well as analysis of response times.

Reports

Labor analysis. The labor report collects information from the call handling system to produce an individual or group-oriented personnel time sheet for any selected range of dates and servicers. It provides information such as work undertaken, arrival dates and times, completion dates and times, time-on-site, traveling time, mileage, and an overall assessment of each servicer, including a statement of hours of overtime unaccounted for. This report makes the task of the payroll department easier and takes away the need for separate weekly time sheets for engineers or vehicles.

Performance analysis. This report can be produced for any given range of dates on the calls received during that period. It shows whether they were completed or remained active; numbers of calls not completed as a result of the first visit; their percentages as a total of all calls; how many calls were completed in one visit, two visits and three or more visits; the total number of site visits necessary within a given time period; how many hours on site; average miles per call; total travel hours for the period; and average travel hours per call.

Financial analysis. Reported costs include repair time, travel time, mileage, costs of parts, total costs, and revenue. The financial analysis report assists sound planning and permits financial comparisons against competitive service offerings.

Parts usage analysis.   Information for each call is produced, within a given area, showing log number, relevant recalls, quantity of parts used, whether parts were used or exchanged, charged or non-chargeable, and their cost and revenue.

Installed base analysis.   Installed base reports can be accessed either by customer, contract, site, or item. These reports predict rate of growth or decline of products, thereby helping the service manager to anticipate staffing and parts requirements. Installed base reports are prompted by a product code range and contract end date, giving details of product codes and descriptions, and month-by-month requirements for signed contracts.

Report generator.   The help desk report generator software prompts the operator to provide a range of information in table format. By entering information concerning customer contract, site number, product code, contract item, engineer, fault code, and the sorting sequence, performance comparisons can be obtained. The system can generate subtotals for each requested category.

Management reports.   Help desk software should provide a comprehensive range of reports to enable managers to become fully informed about the organization's efficiency, profitability, and effectiveness. They can take intelligent action based on up-to-the-minute, accurate information.

Data security.   Help desk software should have its own internal security system, which can be implemented by the customer at initial installation and revised later as necessary. Entry into the system or access to certain information on the system can be limited to a particular branch, or specifically authorized personnel, offices, or geographical areas.

Chapter
18

Needs Analysis

*H*ELP DESK SYSTEMS CONTROL THE SERVICE PROCESSES. They directly affect productivity, quality, customer satisfaction, and profits. Choosing a service system should be a decision made by service management as well as senior management. While service managers must be involved, it is not a decision to be made by them alone.

Needs Analysis

Besides understanding the service environment, it is also important to know the information requirements of the service situation and company. This information is not limited to computer-generated data; it can mean any data that are required to perform an action or accomplish a task. The information may come from computerized or manual processes. Each functional organization involved in service requires information and produces it either for its own consumption or to serve other functions, either within the company or outside it.

The objective is to understand what information is needed, where it is needed, at what time, at what frequency, and in what format. While this seems simple and straightforward, it is not.

There are always combinations and permutations of methods used to transfer information. These include word of mouth, handwritten forms or reports, typed material, tape, floppy disks, and electronic media. The characteristics of each of these forms of communication are different. The help desk project manager must also know how the proposed service system will fit into the overall information strategy and the number and types of interfaces that will be required.

Another reason for learning about the user's organization is to understand the philosophy of service management and its effect on information requirements and on the media employed to acquire and use that information. This knowledge will be used by the system developer for a solution that is more familiar, more comfortable, for the user. The help desk project manager also needs this information to better organize and manage the project.

In modern business, politics have assumed a negative value, overlooking the fact that every organization has politics, with a form and manner of administration that has been deemed essential to the success of the organization. As in any government, a company runs by a series of operating principles—written or unwritten, formal or informal. Such codes and beliefs are the backbone of every corporate culture and are manifest in the policies and the people who administer them. Politics for many people implies bias, prejudices, opinions, and bureaucracy. But politics can also refer to the convictions and opinions held by the members of the user's organization. It is necessary for the system builder and his team to understand what these views are and how they were arrived at. Without any understanding of the culture of the organization for which the system is being planned, project development is virtually impossible.

There are people in any organization who, for a wide variety of reasons, are opposed to change and the agents of change. They can and will do almost anything to keep the status quo. To be aware of opposition and different opinions within the organization is prudent and necessary. With this in mind, it is helpful to choose as project managers people who not only understand service and software technology but who are also skilled in organizational dynamics. Project managers should be able to take a detached view of causes of frustration and remain calm in the face of daily disasters.

Understanding the User Environment

We have learned that there are a number of situations that indicate a troubled service operation. Among them are:

→ No goals

→ No clear management structure

→ No business plans

→ Missing or redundant organizational/operational space procedures

→ No ownership for calls

→ No operating metrics

Any one of these situations is evidence of an organization in need of a service management system.

We have also learned that if you spell out the sort of people you need on your team, by function and by skill level, you can minimize problems. There should be a common level of competency and technical knowledge among the team members. In other words, the team should consist of peers.

It is necessary for a help desk manager to be sensitive to the chain of command. A matrix type of organization will be more receptive to project milestones based on a network of interdependencies. When structuring real time help desks, it is critical to eliminate ambiguity concerning tasks and responsibilities. A particularly skilled and experienced help desk manager is required to maintain strict schedule controls. A service operation with a hierarchical structure and layered management will require a similar organization of tasks and responsibilities. The operations will flow smoothly if the help desk manager does not fight the user's system of management.

Developing a Requirements Document

In any concurrent development, the help desk manager must be the one who develops requirements. Even though the user may have provided a preliminary set of requirements, it is essential that an evaluation team conduct their own study to identify and analyze the logic, the way the system is to be used, and its operational requirements. The resulting document may be called a functional requirement document.

As the help desk project moves through the study, the evaluation team helps develop a blueprint to document the relationships and dependencies between each and every module. The whole point of doing an in-depth study is that the people who will describe, evaluate and use the resultant system will have an intimate understanding of what is needed, why it is needed, who needs it, and exactly how it should work. Having any other group perform such work defeats the purpose of the analysis.

Sometimes, service engineers or support groups will aid in preparing the needs analysis. These people (or even independent consultants) may be called in to develop the requirements.

A typical outline of a requirements specification document should cover:

- Business and system objectives

- Solution requirements

- Logical and physical aspects of the solution

- Scope of solution

- A soluton strategy

- Alternatives and cost benefit analysis

In examining each of these areas, the help desk system manager and his team will acquire a better understanding of the specific problems to address. In the process of learning more about the user's environment, the project team will have determined who will use the system and how it should be used. This information is necessary in order to acquire a system that matches the skills and knowledge of the people who will be responsible for running and supervising the service operation process and making the system accessible to other service personnel. The decision of who will be responsible for building the specifications for the software can also be made at this time.

The help desk manager should be aware that some systems integrators will undertake a requirements analysis with a solution already in mind. It is not surprising, then, to find that what the systems integrator recommends just happens to be what he is selling.

Business goals provide an ongoing focus and incentive for the development process itself. Business goals provide a concrete way to measure whether the system really increases the company's profits. They are also useful metrics when design trade-offs have to be made. The service system can be partitioned so that each element has a one-to-one relationship with the business goals. Having clear, measurable targets can prevent the system vendors from wandering too far from the initial objectives. With business goals, both service managers and senior managers have a more tangible understanding of technical functionality and its associated costs and benefits. It is necessary to know, for example, if more than one service menu could be handled by the proposed system. While the user initially may be concerned only with problems associated with one particular process designed for one specific service, it is often desirable and usually possible to find a system that will include an entire family of products.

The practice of assigning costs to specific services is common. This imposes heavy overhead costs on new services, particularly those with short life cycles or those aimed at niche markets. Knowing that many services can share one process technology is something that has direct bearing on business objectives.

Depending on the complexity of the service delivery process, a requirements study will take anywhere from three to thirty weeks. The study involves interviewing key people in the user's organization, collecting and analyzing relevant data, and looking for ways to maximize the system's effectiveness. This is yet another important reason for having the help desk project manager oversee the requirements study. The help desk manager will review the service process from two perspectives: first, to understand how and why the system functions as it does; second, to determine whether the sequence of events can be altered to achieve greater system throughput or efficiency.

Addressing the Problem

Few real time systems are designed and built using common methodologies in help desk software. In many help desks it is still common to find monolithic real time software that has not been integrated, is not modular, and is therefore extremely difficult to work with (and impossible to change). Industry standards have also largely been ignored.

A service delivery process needs to be examined so that each area may be seen and examined first as a separate entity and then in conjunction with the whole system. This must be done if any kind of model or prototype is to be tried. When this approach is used, the vendor will start with the simplest possible solution and add complexity a module at a time. This method of prescribing systems allows both the vendor and the user to understand the behavior and relationships of functions without creating "spaghetti" code.

The help desk system must be carefully examined so that each layer of functionality is distinct. Integrating modules makes it possible to begin defining the system's attributes based on the requirements, so that various modules become more tangible. Integration provides other benefits such as reducing redundant input.

In every service system concept, there is a core level of functions or modules that is always present regardless of what the process is. The specifics of these functions and how they are arranged and balanced are what make each system different.

All service systems contain a module that triggers or starts the system. Many are based on call handling. A few—very few—are centered around obligation management, or the business arrangement between customer and service provider.

Anticipating Change

The user defines how a system will be used. The help desk manager needs to understand the user's requirements and the environment in which he operates so that he can recommend a system flexible enough to serve current and future needs. The help desk manager is successful when he can match the user's requirements with the best technologies available, in the best possible way to meet the user's business goals.

Chapter

19

Make or Buy?

*A*BOUT EIGHTY PERCENT OF ALL COMPUTER OPERATIONS have already automated their help desk technology or are contemplating doing so in the near future. While there are a growing number of viable help desk software packages, some companies have been reluctant to consider anything other than a "home-grown" product. Paradoxically, a number of organizations have developed in-house service software technology only to outgrow it for one reason or another. These groups are now looking for more flexibility, integration, and capabilities, and are now much more interested in converting to a solutions-oriented vendor-supplied packaged system that incorporates those attributes missing from their original technology.

The functional charters of management information technology shops vary appreciably. There is not much affinity, understanding, or communication between field service and information technology people. Historically, service has been treated as a stepchild by the rest of the company. It has become difficult for service departments to get upper management to understand that customer service can be a real business, as opposed to a mere department. Service requirements for in-house resources generally take a low priority. Data processing technology analysis and programming resources are no different. They are usually scarce for all, but they are especially so for field service.

As service managers plead their case for automating help desks, information technology managers are gradually recognizing the real benefit an automated system imparts. They are beginning to build their own rationale to company management for establishing a separate appropriation to meet service needs, including money for both hardware and personnel. But it takes a long time from inception; by the time help desk technology has been designed, service groups have developed their own information technology function within the service ranks. What follows, usually, is a perpetual building, correcting, modifying, and supporting of the field service help desk systems.

It is only natural for the IT manager responsible for integrating and overseeing his company's automated technology to want to control the activity in-house. He feels compelled to write the code for the technology internally, even if a better solution exists outside the company. However, in our current economic environment, where companies and departments are being down/right sized, many IT managers are opting for outside assistance.

Another important aspect of procuring a help desk management package instead of building one from scratch is that such a package, developed by able vendors, contains enhancements, features, and benefits from a variety of actual users. It represents hundreds of man-years of knowledge and experience. The system developed in-house sacrifices collective experience for customization, often requiring the system's architect to reinvent the wheel. A number of packaged program solutions for field service management technology have been developed based on industry requirements. They are immediately available and, in the long run, are less costly than in-house products.

The decision-making scenario usually ends at the CEO's office or at the senior vice president level, because the IT function and management structure are not the same as the field service upper management. A debate between the service executive team and the systems technology executive team takes place, with the company president as moderator. The issue, of course, is whether to make or buy the service solution. Stronger personalities, politics, and other nonfactual data often affect the final decision. Table 19-1 summarizes the pros and cons to be considered when deciding whether to make or buy a service technology.

Table 19-1 Pros and cons in deciding whether to make or buy help desk management technology

CONS		PROS	
Make	*Buy*	*Make*	*Buy*
Conforms to in-house standard	Immediately available	Expensive	Lacks customization
Dedicated support	Industry proven	Extra-long start-up	Independent
Runs on existing hardware	Less costly	Competes with other management information technology projects—forever	Not easily modified
Customized to user's specific needs	Quicker return on investment	Ultimately more costly	Requires conversion from current system
	Incorporates experience and multiple user enhancements		

Table 19-2 Reasons for developing in-house or buying a help desk management system

Reason	Rank Among Those Currently Considering Use	Rank Among Current Users
Available Resources	1	4
Unavailable Resources	2	1
No time to develop	3	5
Vendor package too expensive	4	6
Found a system we liked	5	2

1 = Most Important
Source: Independent research

An industry leader in packaged help desk management technology spent over $15 million in developing its well-known help desk management system. An analysis of the resources and effort required to develop the system demonstrates the commitment and resources required to do the job right. It is summarized in Table 19-3. This information seems to justify the need to fully evaluate the help desk application marketplace before making the decision to grow your own system.

Table 19-3 Commitment and resources required to develop a help desk management system

Module	Number of Programs	Thousands of Lines of Code	Man Years of Effort
Call Handling	1690	586	50
Administrative	514	164	10
Parts Management	1396	503	41

In every IT organization there are software engineers who want to design their own real time systems. The principal argument for allowing them to do so is that they can "save the company a lot of money." The problem is that in-house people are, by their very position, isolated from the vast body of knowledge required to not only become a competent architect but also to remain one. Homegrown systems put an immediate barrier between system architect and end user and guarantee that the requirements are not open to inspection or analysis. It will take six months to a year to create a patchwork system out of different homegrown solutions; what is more, the system will lack flexibility and modularity, be very hard to change, difficult to maintain, and probably end up costing more.

Homegrown systems inevitably lack flexibility and modularity and almost always cost more money. To be truly effective, a system must be easy to run, easy to maintain, easy to change, and easy to upgrade. The architect must be able to anticipate changes in computer architectures, operating systems, programming languages, network topologies, communications protocols, and changes in supporting equipment, such as logistics systems.

There is another manifestation of the homegrown solution that is more common and perhaps more troublesome. It is certainly more costly. It occurs when someone tries to use a number of commercial software packages to build a system in less time and with lower costs. Real time software systems are quite different from other types of software. They are more critical to a company's success than database or word processing software. They have a greater impact in a shorter period of time on the profitability of a company.

Chapter

20

Choosing a Software Package and Vendor

Preliminary Contact

W HEN VENDORS ARE CONTACTED FOR HELP DESK LITERA-
TURE, their sales effort is launched. Salesmen will descend. A
preliminary meeting may occur, therefore, sometime during the
pre-selection process, although it may not be the best time for
a visit. In the first place, the vendors have not been narrowed,
and the help desk project team is, therefore, spending time with
a vendor who may not be in the final list. In addition, if this is
the case, it may well be a waste of time for the vendor and user
as well. In this regard, it has always seemed better to delay
the vendor visits until all the key requirements and functional
specification have been documented and approved and the list
of vendor candidates has been prepared. The team then invites
the vendors, having prepared specific questions relating to the
software package to be evaluated.

The best approach is to write a letter to potential vendors
that clearly sets forth the objectives of the selection project and a
statement of the key functional requirements and non-functional

requirements—such as response time—that are not apparent from the source literature. This provides the vendor with some direction for the meeting.

Preparing an agenda for the meeting is also wise and helpful. The meeting, which should be attended by all selection team members and, if possible, key steering committee members, should consist of the following agenda:

- Introduction of team members and their positions. Including a person's title and position helps the vendor focus his presentation on areas of interest to his audience.

- Restatement, from the letter, of the objective and key requirements.

- Vendor presentation of his product.

- Questions from the audience relating to specific requirements and how the software package will address each.

- Closing remarks.

It should be understood, at this point in the selection process, that the vendor's presentation must be general; he does not yet understand the intricacies of the audience's company, policies, and procedures. He will begin with a description of his company, including history, size, locations, market thrust, and other information that will provide insight into his organization. However, the meeting will be more productive for both user and vendor if the user restates his hot button to the vendor

Questions from the audience should be structured to help define how the system will work in their own environment. This approach will provide tremendous insight into the critical question of "fit" and will begin to give the team a picture of the degree of modifications that will be required. This degree of fit, of course, must be clearly defined before making a final selection.

Closing remarks, by the selection team leader, should provide the vendor with the next steps. For example, the team leader may advise the vendor that several other vendors will be invited to make presentations over the next few weeks. Or he may want to introduce the idea of site visits so the vendor can begin to plan for the visits. He should then clearly define the parameters of the visits, such as type of industry, geographic preferences, time frames, and other such logistical matters.

During these initial visits the selection team should be well prepared with questions directed to their unique requirements. In addition, they should look for nuances in different approaches, styles, and levels of professionalism. Some vendors are eliminated in this process. This is particularly true for those who cannot address the key functional requirements of the selecting company. After these visits, the team can begin to designate the final candidates. This process and the ones that follow are like peeling back the onion skin to increasingly more detail.

In summary, the help desk system buyer should anticipate several things in these vendor visits. Independent software vendors may be flip and illusive about the capabilities of their systems. Few will acknowledge a poor fit at this early stage. All will try to get to the next phase with a proposal and an invitation to visit the selecting company's offices. Few will seek to have the potential customer prepare a request for proposal, which will be discussed later. Caution should be exercised when vendors claim they can "do it all."

Final Candidates

Final candidates should be selected at this point, and the documented analysis should be presented to the steering committee. If even one of the vendors invited to make an initial presentation is eliminated for good cause, the effort will have paid for itself. The next steps in the selection process are frequently time consuming and may entail travel and related other costs. As the final list evolves, the selection team should so advise the vendors. At this time, the team should request a list of sites to visit and schedule a visit to the vendor. Each of these tasks is discussed below.

Visits to the Vendor

In the process of making the final selection, the selection team should visit the vendor. There are several specific reasons for this visit. They include evaluation of the vendor's management and commitment; demonstration of the system being evaluated; and an opportunity to view the vendor's facilities and support capability. Evaluation of the vendor's management and its commitment is not an in-depth psychological appraisal. It is a time to observe management's interest. The level of interest shown by the vendor may well foretell the level and intensity of support down the road. Impressions are very important here. Sometimes vendor visits warrant several days. In these cases, there will be a lot of intense dialogue and learning, on both sides. As in academia, it is a good idea to set aside at least a half day in the visit for a strictly social outing local sightseeing, golf game or the like.

Demonstration

The stated purpose of a meeting with a vendor, of course, is to see a demonstration of his system. Normally, vendors will have a demonstration or test case that can be used to test the system.

First, user friendliness will be very apparent from the demonstration. Cluttered screens with too much information are easily seen. Inadequate or clumsy use of menus will be readily apparent. Inefficient use of command keys and the cursor would be other indicators of poor systems work. These will be clear from a demonstration. Second, the existence of bugs or programming logic errors will be obvious. Third, poor response time for entering transactions cannot be hidden or downplayed by the vendor and his demonstrator. Fourth, violations of common business conventions will jump out when they occur, indicating that the system may not be appropriate in your environment.

Other observations that can be provided from a demonstration will require probing. In this, the team should have some specific "how do you handle this" type questions for the vendor. In all fairness, these questions should be held to the end of the presentation. Interjecting these questions during the demonstration is disruptive and most often results in a "wait and see" response from the vendor.

Operating Scenarios

It is recommended that the help desk project team prepare a set of live operating scenarios which reflect actual business practices and ask the vendor to incorporate them into the demo presentation. These case studies should obviously be given to the vendor in advance of the visit so he will have time to prepare his response. Often the vendor response to your actual case will reveal his ability to meet your overall need.

Financial Strength

The team can get some idea of the viability of the vendor, which is, of course, important. It is important to remember that there are many small companies in the service management systems industry, and the failure rate is high. You do not want to select a vendor who then goes into Chapter 11 or merely disbands.

Financial strength is not, of course, a negative factor with the major hardware manufacturers who market applications software. It is probably not of any concern when dealing with the premier software vendors. Financial position probably should be of concern when dealing with a vast majority of the software vendors now in the market. It is appropriate to request annual statements from publicly held companies and financial statements from privately held firms. The advice here is clear: however possible, the selection team had better assure itself of the viability of the selected vendor. The best time for this is during the visit to the vendor's location.

Service

The selection team can evaluate the company's facilities and the strength of its support quite easily during this visit. Adequate facilities should include, at a minimum, hardware to support continuing development and enhancement of the system (although development for hardware manufacturers will not be at a district or regional office), and training facilities with user terminals and teacher terminals that can be easily seen through rear projection or communications with the user terminals. These can be quickly assessed by the selection team. Technical support can be assessed as well. A walk through of the vendor's own help desk facility might prove interesting. While offering an indication of how it handles support requests, it might also provide you with some refreshing ideas which you could incorporate. The primary issue here is the number and geographic location of the software maintenance (systems engineers) personnel. Experience says that you should pay little heed to "800" toll-free debuggers/problem solvers or to remote diagnostics. These services have seldom been effective, although they sound modern and sophisticated. Perhaps there are software vendors who can offer efficient and effective support remotely, but they are the exceptions. The more critical question is, How many technical representatives/software maintenance personnel are available for your company?

Are Reference Visits Necessary?

A legitimate question could be raised as to the necessity and value of reference site visits. Prior to the predominance of service software packages, there was little need to visit a prospective vendor. In those days, in-house developed systems were designed for the requirements of the user, and the existence of another, similar, system was not really that important (or that easy to find).

Visiting a site today, where a particular package of interest is installed, is much like taking a new car for a drive—it is supposed to determine, as best as possible, how the system works in a real live environment. It is worth the effort and highly recommended if properly done. There are two important things to keep in mind while preparing for reference visits. First, you should select sites that most nearly approximate your business and environment. Second, you should prepare an agenda and a list of questions that an experienced user would best know how to answer—for instance, Is it easy to use? Does it slow down in peak periods? Does it provide good audit trails and management reports?

Reference Site Selection

Quite naturally, vendors are prone to recommend their most successful implementations and those that will earn then good reviews. Some users, however, really enjoy demonstrating their systems and do good jobs of it. The best way, therefore, to try and get an objective view is to specify the type of company the selection team would like to see. Specifically, the selection team may request a complete list of a prospective vendor's customers, and they may specify:

→ The exact industry

→ Company size in terms of numbers of people or sales volumes

→ Geography, if it is relevant in terms of experience with support

→ Years of experience with the system if new versions are frequent

At this point in the selection process, the team can be aggressive but reasonable in its demands.

Agenda

An agenda is helpful in assisting the vendor set up your appointment and in communicating your expectations for the proposed visit.

SAMPLE AGENDA

9:00–10:00	Meet with Service Management
10:00–10:30	Review Contract Administration
10:30–11:00	Review Call Handling
11:00–11:30	Review Logistics
11:30–12:30	Summary with general manager
Lunch	Paid by visitor/vendor

A visit may require a full day, but the host customer may be unwilling to devote that much time. The selection team should not despair, as quite a lot can be accomplished in half a day if the team is well prepared for the visit.

The team should clearly set forth its objectives in requesting a visit. While on site, however, you should look around for indicators that have nothing to do with your proposed objectives. For instance, big piles of uncompleted input forms on worker's desks probably indicate poor response time. Manuals lying around probably belie ease of use. Call handlers watching screens but not entering data indicate inactive call handlers. Finally, having clerks working on procedures—rather than a specialist—indicates lack of support. There are obviously many more areas of concern and related indicators that can be discussed before the visit. There also should be sets of questions for the users and technical staff. Questions to the host user should be directed toward user friendliness, ease of installation, and support.

With such a well-planned excursion, the selection team will greatly benefit and take another important step toward final selection. It has become somewhat normal for a selection team to visit at least two locations. At the same time, probably no more than three locations should be visited.

Selection Criteria

As stated earlier, there are two major considerations when buying any products or service. The first and perhaps the most important is the vendor company itself: its stability, size, flexibility, profitability, capabilities, track record, and future viability. The vendor's understanding of the market and his ability to listen to and respond to the needs of his customers and prospects are critical. The other consideration, of course, is the product itself—from the standpoint of functionality, flexibility, capability, support, ease of installation, and reliability.

You might consider using the following checklist* for selecting service software.

Table 20-1A Vendor selection criteria checklist

Vendor Financial Strength _____
VENDOR NAME _____

	Amount	Comments
Sales	$ _____	_____
Assets	$ _____	_____
Working capital	$ _____	_____
Profitability	$ _____	_____
Research and development	$ _____	_____
Stock price and trend	$ _____	_____
Credit rating	$ _____	_____

Table 20-1B Vendor Selection Criteria Checklist

VENDOR ORGANIZATION

Employees	Number	Comments
Management and administration	_____	_____
Sales and Marketing	_____	_____
Customer support	_____	_____
Product planning	_____	_____
Product development	_____	_____
Quality assurance	_____	_____
Documentation	_____	_____
Training	_____	_____
Consulting	_____	_____
Other	_____	_____

1. Determine the global objectives and feasibility of the proposed system; gain approval to proceed.

2. Determine the functional (needs) specifications.

3. Identify any constraints you have on hardware selection.

---

*Source: Dr. William Evers

Table 20-1C Vendor Selection Criteria Checklist

BASIC COMPANY CHARACTERISTICS

Company characteristics (management characteristics, style, professionalism, image, etc.)

_____

_____

Number of years in business _____
Background of executives

CEO _____

_____

President

_____

_____

VPs

_____

_____

Others

_____

_____

Company outlook

_____

_____

Table 20-1D Vendor Selection Criteria Checklist

VENDOR CLIENTELE

Number of installations _____
Industries in client base
Electronics _____
Plant Engineering _____
Medical Equipment _____
Government _____
Communications _____
3rd Party Maintenance _____
Others _____
Active user group? Purpose and function

_____

_____

Table 20-1E Vendor Selection Criteria Checklist

VENDOR ASSESSMENT

Referenceable client list

_____

_____

Summary
Financial: _____
Organization: _____
Clientele: _____

Overall Assessment:

_____

_____

_____

Table 20-2 Product-based selection criteria checklist

Overall System Requirements	Rating
User friendliness	_____
Expendability (business growth and technology)	_____
Easy-to-follow documentation	_____
Easily accessible audit traits	_____
Organizational and geographical rollups	_____
A quick and easy access to multiple screens and files	_____
Quick response	_____
Menu-driven operations	_____
Automated preventive maintenance	_____
Technical and manpower utilization data collection system	_____
Warranty and nonwarranty service	_____

Database Requirements	Rating
Equipment inventory control	_____
Customer/account control	_____
Service engineer roster	_____

4. Obtain a complete vendor list.

5. Use a screening process to rule out those vendor offerings that are unacceptable.

6. Issue a request for information.

7. Develop a vendor/needs matrix.

8. Explore user experience with qualified vendors.

9. Calculate total costs to install the system.

10. Select the best package based on cost, quality, and performance.

11. Negotiate with the vendor.

Chapter

21

Implementing a Help Desk System

*A*FTER THE SYSTEMS VENDOR HAS BEEN CHOSEN THE REAL WORK BEGINS. Usually the help desk project team, the group that selected the software system is charged with the responsibility of implementing that new software into its help desk. At this stage, buyer's remorse may be prevalent as the team sets out to change the world of the many folks who have worked hard to understand and use the old system intelligently. This is when the "tree huggers" really make themselves known.

Tasked with the implementation of the new system, the help desk project team will be faced initially with what may appear to be a very unreasonably tight schedule from management. The switch from evaluating the package to formulating how it will work in its new surroundings is a crucial passage. First of all, the team knows that the package will not accommodate one hundred percent of its needs—no package ever does. They must look at the areas that need to be "customized" to fit their particular situation. This "gap" analysis can expose questionable or perhaps even redundant business practices, which could be changed more readily than altering or adding to source code. The task is to determine the overall fit and see how successfully the new system will function. This period offers an ideal time for the new help desk system users and managers to clean house and re-engineer their practices, policies and procedures to achieve a better, more productive *modus operandi*.

To implement a new software package successfully it is necessary to analyze current operations in detail. By comparing the new system with the old one, the level of effort to implement both the easy components and the more difficult ones can be established.

It is likely that Mr. Pareto's law will prevail in the implementation exercise, since about one-fifth of most implementations produce four-fifths of all the problems. Assigning ownership and responsibility and outlining a realistic project schedule for the implementation are also essential. Assessing current procedures and operations and regularly checking progress against goals and objectives are critical. The process requires a separate plan for each module of the package. Initial planning should include naming and organizing the implementation teams and meeting with them for orientation and review of strategy and methodology.

Going back and just reviewing the old systems and procedures is a data collection effort which can be massive if housekeeping and chronicles had been handled in a sloppy fashion. The information is used to assess the impact of new systems installation. Hopefully, most of this information will have been gathered already during the selection phases of the project. Data include workflows, organization, input media, reports, processing schedules, forms, resources, business practices, and procedures, to name a few. The information is also used later to assess the magnitude and complexity of data conversion, training and organizational changes. Constantly checking progress against goals, objectives and project scope helps reveal the near- and long-term shortcomings and benefits derived from the new software vis a vis the current system. This ongoing appraisal alerts the organization to potential impact of operational, technical, and control processes which will change as a result of the new package.

Validation

Validating the new package involves matching it to the current system and requires the collection of data that will be needed during the installation and ongoing maintenance phases of the project. The single most important reason for this documentation is to eventually compare it to the flow of the new application software system. It is the means to determine the fit definitively, before the implementation actually begins. It is also the way to humanize the system as we begin to see how the real people will use this new phenomenon and to consummate the transfer of ownership to the user teams and eventually the end-user. Validation includes the documentation of procedures, reports, forms, and other business tools that will be used to assess the effort required to convert data from manual or computerized files to the new system's file structure. The degree of training required and any need for further organizational changes will be determined from the information gathered during this important analytic process.

Live data is captured, evaluated, and made part of the ongoing implementation documentation. Special effort is made to identify and resolve situations that would adversely impact the planned installation.

The validation activity also provides the transition from the "plan" to the "live" result before any major amount of inconvenience is encountered. The reality of actual, specific data is used to check the completeness and workability of the plans that have been generated. And as real data is collected, some conflicts are likely to appear. Resolution early in the process will allow for smoother flow during installation. In many cases the customer will need to be an active player in clearly defining exact requirements and suggesting or approving solutions.

Any benchmark, test-bed or development system that might be installed is done during the validation period and allows for shakedown of any special testing or installation procedures that have been developed. Any internal, cross-functional service delivery dependencies are identified and resolved on a team basis.

Validation is completed when data has been collected and the various plans that will be used during the installation and operations phases have been legitimately finalized. The users of the system are the ultimate validators. It is important that they accept the various plans and system solution being implemented. In many cases management will be looking for information that shows that the situation is under control and that potential crisis areas have been identified and addressed. Others may want very detailed processes written and presented to them.

The Team

The selection team now becomes the implementation project team, more or less. Some new members may be added and some old members may leave the team. The management committee involved in selecting the evaluation team and approving the project and funding it also should remain in tact, mainly to provide the overall direction of the implementation effort. Normally, the makeup of the management committee does not change at all. Specifically, the management committee is responsible for confirmation of corporate goals and objectives, establishing financial and human resource commitments, and approval at critical phases and decision points throughout the project. All organizations affected by the new system would be represented on implementation project team, including those employees who will operate the help desk system (customer service), control the system (IT), and are responsible for the system (end-user).

Specialty subgroups representing different areas of the business, such as logistics and product support, for example, should also be included in the project team. Each user should also have a representative on the project team. The consolidation of cross-functional subgroups under the direction of one director/team member may be necessary. One person is selected as project leader, obviously. This, in many cases, is the leader of the selection team. However, the implementation project team should be driven by the person who has the best overall grasp of the total project. This individual is the one who is usually the most difficult to obtain because of the importance of his normal duties. More successful implementations include the user teams with specific responsibilities to implement the modules they will own. The scope of the system, in terms of modules, should now be clearly established.

Adequate representation by the IT department is a must and sometimes it is the IT manager who drives the project team. The advantage of this is that the IT manager is project-oriented and is normally trained in project management techniques. Historically, of course, the difficulty here has been that users have abdicated their responsibilities and considered the system as an IT system rather than a user system. This is disastrous and one of the major reasons that software implementations sometimes fail.

The challenge here is to clearly understand the delegation of duties between the implementation project team and the user implementation teams. The responsibilities of the project leader and his team are enumerated below.

Developing the master implementation plan:

— Organize and manage the team.

— Produce and monitor master schedule.

— Train the user implementation teams.

— Review and approve detailed user plans.

— Design and incorporate a reporting scheme.

— Monitor and manage the project.

— Plan the installation of the system.

— Orchestrate company-wide education and training.

— Orchestrate conversion plans.

There is an underlying strategy that is quite important here. The implementation project team *really doesn't do anything*. Look at its charter. It plans, approves, recommends, monitors, coordinates, schedules and organizes. *Planning and monitoring* the efforts of the user implementation team is the secret to avoiding implementation trouble.

What then do the user implementation teams do? *Everything*, as shown below:

— Develop *detailed* implementation plans.

— Provide accurate, comprehensive and timely reports.

— Document current systems and procedures.

— Benchmark the new environment.

— Develop all user procedures.

— Educate and train all users.

— Plan and incorporate unique conversions.

— Authorize and monitor any customizations.

— Cut over to "live" system operations.

It should be clear now that the user teams will request and need assistance from the IT staff continuously along the way. A perfect example is the need to have programming assistance in any conversion programs and in making modifications to the software.

Implementation Resources

Resources need to be committed for a successful implementation. This means that all the tasks, documentation, commitments and schedules required to make sure that the team is completely ready to implement the new package are in place. What type of skills are needed? Where? When? Who is going to provide them? Does the specific person who is going to deliver the skill even know about this project? Is he trained, does he have the right materials on hand, and know where to go, whom to see, what to do, and when to do it?

Verification of source commitments is a critical task of the team. Schedules are required from each group supporting the implementation. All arrangements and contact lists, including individual names and phone numbers, have to be finalized with the team with firm schedule dates for any preparation work that needs to be done. These apply to all modules, vendors and various geographical areas that are involved.

While the resource commitment stage tends to be an ongoing operational issue, it is theoretically finished when the installation takes place. For practical purposes, resources are under control when they have been identified and committed and are firmly on schedule.

The Master Implementation Plan

The entire project must be planned to include each user implementation plan. But this master plan is the responsibility of the implementation project team. It is not always easy. A major concern is deciding on the best sequence for installing multiple modules or even multiple functions within a single module. In the former, the team must plan the sequence for obligation management, call handling, logistics, product support, purchasing and finance, to name a few. The master implementation plan is a comprehensive collection of all documentation, procedures, schedules, and contact lists needed in the new package. It makes use of the detailed checklist that was developed during the validation. It contains individual user plans for each aspect of the project.

Really, the on-going master implementation plan is a "living" document that needs continual updating as events, places and people change.

The following outline includes some suggestions for organizing the many different types of information that might be needed within a project:

1) Project information, such as overviews, project manager's role, who's who, project plan and timeline, schedule overview, summary of critical documents, security, health, safety statements, goals and objectives.

2) Contact lists

3) Event schedules. In a large project, many events will be happening simultaneously around the country and/or world. At times it will be difficult to keep track of what has to happen next, or even what is supposed to be happening now. The project manager needs to establish some form of "tickler" system that flags important schedule events ahead of time, and with enough lead time for correction if it is off schedule.

4) Technical plans and documenti;

5) Resources

6) Document/Report/Update Storage. The need to keep individual reports and/or documents is dictated by each program. It is possible to have the need to look up facts, commitments or reports years after they occurred.

Because of the large quantity of information, it may be advantageous to create summaries of the various plans contained within the ongoing master plan. These summaries can be used for an overview of events and processes.

The sequence of implementing multiple functions or modules is almost always a consideration, because normally the company or organization simply cannot handle all of the change at one time. Therefore, modules are implemented at the pace the user can absorb; and this must be planned. Most help desk vendors, unfortunately, do not provide guidance on sequence. The best source of assistance is a new breed of company in the information service industry that specializes in implementations. The Cobre Corporation of New Jersey is an example.

The master plan establishes the time frame for each implementation team and for the user plans. The master plan should include those tasks that are generic to the project and those that cross the lines of two or more user teams. The master plan first establishes the total project life cycle and the time frames and sequence of implementation of the individual user modules. Thereafter, the plan should include those areas listed under the responsibilities of the project implementation teams. The project leader should set time frames for developing the individual user plans, the software installation, the schedules for conversion, the cutover and the post-assessment.

Kickoff Meetings

The project leader and his team should schedule kickoff meetings with users and with the new implementation teams as part of the master plan. (Much of this content should have been covered in the selection process.) New members of the team, who were not members of the selection team, should meet with the project leader to review the selection process, management's decision to proceed, and the basics of the new system to be implemented. The project leader should, at this meeting, review the overall implementation plan, answering questions and providing the rationale for the approach.

A meeting with the users must be planned carefully and scheduled strategically; that is, not on a Friday afternoon or before a three-day weekend. There are several approaches to this, but one basic requirement is essential to each approach: management must be present to bless the effort, establish its support, and request the cooperation of all users who must implement the system and be its eventual users. Two common approaches to this user kickoff may be helpful in planning.

Plenary meeting. One approach is to have a single plenary meeting of all key department heads and users. In this format, management opens the meeting with the commitments discussed above. The project leader discusses the overall systems, the goals, and the strategy. It is important to introduce any outside consultants, as well, and to explain their roles in the project. Users should be invited to ask questions in an open discussion. This should not, however, get into the details of how the system itself will work. This could take days and the project team is not really prepared at this stage to answer this level of detailed questioning.

User meetings. An alternative, with the very same agenda, is to have a series of meetings with the user users of each module separately. One advantage here is that the project manager can be a little more specific about the individual modules. The agenda, however, should be basically the same, and the same persons should be introduced with an explanation of roles and responsibilities.

The final step in the early stage development of an overall plan is to train the implementation team in certain key tasks they must undertake. Specifically, the teams should be trained in:

- The project management system so they can develop their own implementation plans

- The methodologies to be used in documenting the present functions, developing the new environment for the new system, and preparing user documentation

This is important in that control over the entire project is facilitated when all elements are working from the same game plan and using the same tools and techniques.

User Plans

The teams's first task is to develop individual user plans for their areas of responsibility. These must include the time to document current procedures, gathering relevant current forms, and selecting current reports that will be required of the new system. The teams must estimate the times to define current and new procedures and to prepare user documentation for the new procedures. Next, the teams must estimate times to plan and conduct in-house training. Finally, the teams must determine the extent of life creation and conversion, conference room pilot preparation and execution, and a projection of cutover times. The sources of information for these tasks are vendors, vendor literature, users of the system, and implementation firms. This type of information should be readily available.

Each of the user teams submits its plan to the project leader for review, approval, and consolidation with the other teams' plans. The review establishes the fact that each identified task includes a specific person(s) who is responsible and a specific start and stop date. The individual plans must be consistent and within the specified guidelines and time frames of the overall project plan. The plan is consolidated and published. Interactions between two or more user teams are identified and planned. The project leader reports the plan to the management committee for its approval. The plan is readied for adaptation as a reporting scheme.

Reporting Scheme

The project implementation team should, in the planning phase, evaluate and recommend a reporting scheme. Maintaining the system depends upon the individual user plans being accurate and timely. It should be computerized. Software packages for project management are available on microprocessors and other larger computers. Graphics capabilities are an important element in the package selected for project management. The important features include:

• Ability to set up work breakdown structures and input effort and results against these elements of the plan. Accomplishments and measured results should be easy to see in terms of days on an event and the percentage completion/percentage to complete.

• A facility to force the discipline of analyzing dependencies between tasks and the relationship of tasks and the impact of slippages.

• Milestone chart capabilities to show start, end, and interim review dates.

• Reporting capabilities such as lists of tasks, tasks completed, and tasks in process.

The computerized system is then used to report on a periodic basis to management. A project management system combines networking, resource scheduling, estimating and accounting; and helps locate variances by comparing actual work against the schedule.

All of this can also be handled manually without a computerized project management system; but with the hundreds of tasks associated with the implementation of systems, it seems unproductive to handle these manually and create progress reports manually for the management committee. With the computerized system, many of which cost less than $500, the reporting becomes automatic. Teams report hours and accomplishments by task numbers. The project team inputs the data and produces detail status reports back to the implementation teams; and high-level summary reports to management. The summary reports are by system and module rather than detail task.

Team Reviews

Reviews of individual user plans and documents will occur during the development of each. A final review meeting with appropriate team members and the help desk project implementation manager will help ensure that the master plan is complete and that the scheduling information is accurate.

Schedules change, people move and plans are revised. All changes need to be captured and used to update the master plan. A change control process needs to be developed with the customer and internally so that changes that affect the project will be known by the project manager.

Overseeing the Project Teams

The project team has the responsibility at all times to oversee the overall project. This can be best accomplished by giving all of the responsibility of implementation to the individual user teams. The project team should not assign itself any specific tasks such as documenting flows, developing user procedures, or converting specific files. The project team should provide guidance, resolve conflicts resulting from overlaps of information/responsibilities between two or more teams, oversee the project and report to the management committee.

Mirroring the Objectives

Original objectives must always be reflected by the project and the project team. The only important note here is to recommend that the implementation teams refine its list of potential costs, goals and benefits arising from the documentation of transactions and procedures. It is almost inconceivable that this detailed analysis would not uncover some inconsistencies and inefficiencies that can be addressed during the implementation. It is a time of change. When will there ever be a better time to streamline the organization?

Upon completion of the documentation and refinement of the opportunities for near-and short-term benefits, the teams should compile all of the flowcharts and analyses. These should be submitted to the project leader for monitoring and submission to the management committee. The first important steps to implementation of the software package are behind us. But nothing has changed, yet.

Change Management

At this stage the software should be installed. Vendors install; most of them do not implement. Installing a help desk system can take weeks and is usually an exercise where the vendor brings his diskettes and loads the system onto the computer. The vendor checks screens and menus and declares that the system is ready. As the vendor departs, the team realizes that life will never be the same; they hope it will be better. Now we must understand the extent of the change. Transaction by transaction, the implementation teams must compare the old with the new. Flowcharts must be compared with user flowcharts, which should be provided by the vendor or developed by the user. Input forms must be compared to screens in the new system. Decision points should be discussed and analyzed. Changes in the way the function is performed from the way we do business must be highlighted.

Reports must be analyzed comparing old reports with the reports generated by the new system. Much of this will be completed earlier in the key requirements phase of the selection process. We are now fine-tuning to avoid surprises and eliminate the trauma of the unexpected. We are trying to make the change understood and acceptable. The human element of systems is never more important or all-pervasive as it is during this early phase of implementation of a new system.

The next steps involve a heavy commitment from all concerned. The implementation teams must document the new system and how it will work in the current environment: the final assessment. They must develop user procedures that reflect their company and department. They must plan and execute training under the helpful direction of the project teams. Following these tasks, the teams must develop conversion plans and the project team must coordinate a company-wide conversion plan. The concept of a pilot conference will surface as a way for users to test the system in its entirety. The system goes live and all planning becomes reality.

Finally, the post-implementation assessment must be scheduled, staffed and completed. This is a measurement of the effect and benefits arising from the change. And, throughout it all, we are dealing with the human element and the consequences of change, which never come easy. The best implementations always concentrate on the most important component of the project, that is, the human factor. It is the orientation of the user and the IT team; it is not a technical orientation.

Chapter

22

Return on Investment from a Computerized Help Desk Service Management System

*R*ETURN ON INVESTMENT IS PERCENTAGE RETURN THAT A company can anticipate over the life of a project, based on the timed comparisons between the inflow and outflow of related project funds. We now offer an evaluation guide designed to bring into clear focus the return on investment for the acquisition and implementation of an automated field service management system.

The allocation of project funds by executive management will be based on measurable results, especially where the benefits will be achieved during their management tenure. For service proposals in particular, which tend to be outside the executive management experience sphere, this is favorable because of the high return on investment and short payback periods. Service management must be careful in presenting return on investment benefits so as not to overstate its case.

Benefits must be measurable in an understandable way without straining credibility; they must be capable of ongoing measurements, so that at any time one can take a reliable data reading; and they must be quantifiable at the start of the project. The impact areas identified below form the basis for calculating the return on investment by comparing estimated fund streams for dollar inflows and outflows. These estimates are presented as a guide based on market research with technology-based companies that had manual, semiautomated, or insufficiently automated systems. The calculations have been specified with conservative operating ratios to portray results on a recurring annual basis, to consolidate their impact. This approach also demonstrates that the payback period associated with the return on investment is attractively short. For readers who want to reflect projected differences in fund flow from year to year, a separate return on investment worksheet should be used for each year. Each company's actual measurable numbers and results may differ from the guidelines discussed here.

Calculating Return on Investment

Following is an accounting of specific areas in which savings result from implementing a computerized field service management system. Traditionally, such a system comprises software programs that enable dispatchers to handle their customers' calls for service, the execution and completion of the service actions, and reporting capability to produce field engineer productivity, equipment performance, failure date, and cost/revenue data by person or by product, in multiple geographical and organizational tiers. Auxiliary modules include spare parts provisioning and inventory control as well as billing.

Cash Flow Impact Areas

Call handling and dispatching procedures help increase field service manpower productivity. Computerized call handling reduces nonproductive time (such as travel and waiting) for both the field engineer and dispatch staff. A variety of direct operational measurements are available to substantiate personnel productivity, including revenue/field engineer and machine loading/field engineer. The calculation for productivity improvement is:

$$\textit{(No. Field Engineers + No. Dispatch Staff)} \\ \times \textit{(Average Compensation)} \times \textit{(\% Improvement)}$$

A conservative figure for percentage improvement is 5 percent.

Reduced local and long distance calls (for parts expediting, service engineers' assignments and call backs, for example) can be expected with an integrated field service database. Local answering services can be cancelled. The calculation for cost savings from reduced telephone usage is:

$$\textit{(Annual Apportioned Operations Phone Bill)} \\ \times \textit{Reduction)} + \textit{(Total of Local Phone Answering Service Bills)}$$

Increases in service revenue can occur from identifying accounts that are out of contract to be billed at the time and materials rate, credit holds, or by a timely notification and follow-up for contract renewals:

$$\textit{(Current Maintenance Warranty Revenue)} \times \textit{(\% Improvement)}$$

A conservative figure for percentage improvement is 1%.

Spare parts inventory and logistics systems reduce inventory carrying costs. Cost savings from service systems are achieved by reducing inventory carrying costs (cost of money, space, insurance, etc.) associated with reduced spares levels facilitated by a logistics module. This also builds field confidence in stocked levels, spares location, and produce life cycle kit/spares utilization. The calculation for reduction in carrying costs is:

$$\textit{(Spare Inventory Valuation)} \times \textit{(\% Inventory Reduction)} \; \textit{(\% Carrying Costs)}$$

Conservative figures for percentage reduction and percentage carrying costs are 7 percent and 20 percent, respectively.

Reduction in the need for emergency shipments of spare parts by overnight couriers (with precise parts location identification) is also accommodated by a one-system package:

$$(Annual\ Emergency\ Shipping\ Charges) \times (percentage\ reduction)$$

A conservative figure for perecentage reduction is 25%.

Reduction in time for preparation, review, and approval of the customer's invoice (especially for time and materials billing) results from the logistics module. The calculation for the reduction is:

$$\frac{(Average\ Outstanding\ A/R) \times (Current\ Annual\ Interest\ Rate) \times (Day\ Reduction)}{365}$$

A conservative figure to use for this reduction is 30 days in outstanding accounts receivable.

A worksheet for determining the return on investment is given in Worksheet 22-1.

Table 22-1 Worksheet for determining return on investment

COST SAVINGS

AND PRODUCTIVITY IMPROVEMENT ESTIMATES

ANNUALIZED

Field service productivity (number of field engineers_____
    + number dispatch staff) × (average
    compensation) × 5%
Telephone bill reduction (annual apportioned   _____
    operations phone bill) × 20% + (local phone
    answering services)
Maintenance of time and material revenue (current_____
    maintenance warranty revenue) × 1%
Spare inventory carrying costs (spares inventory   _____
    valuation) × (number of turns) × 7% × 20%
Emergency shipping charges (annual emergency   _____
    shipping charges) × 25%
Invoicing (Average outstanding accounts   _____
    receivable) (current interest rate) − (30)/365
Total cost savings and productivity improvement   _____

Expense Estimates Annualized (excluding software)

Telephone communication equipment   _____
Computer hardware & peripherals   _____
Handheld terminals   _____
Additional expenses   _____
Manpower related to training and database building_____
Total operating expenses   _____

Return on investment + Net operational savings
    Software expenses   =_____

23

Help Desk Case Study: Atlantic Telephone Company

THIS CASE STUDY IS ABOUT A REGIONAL TELEPHONE COM-
PANY, which, for the sake of anonymity, will be called Atlantic
Telephone Company, or Atlantic Tel. Proper nouns used herein
are fictitious. Proprietary information is excluded. The case is
presented in the form of the actual final report that was presented to Atlantic Tel in response to their need for guidance in
planning their help desk, at the definition phase.

This case study is included in this book for the following
reasons:

■ Atlantic Tel intended to differentiate its entire company
from forthcoming competition by building and managing a centralized, steamlined help desk.

■ The new help desk was envisioned by Atlantic Tel to be
the most important medium for customer satisfaction.

■ Almost every department within Atlantic Tel had its own
individual help desk, and there was very little cross-functional
coordination and integration.

Introduction

Atlantic Tel anticipates a significant increase in competition in the near future as a result of court decisions and regulations. Atlantic Tel's president stated that "by staying close to our customers, we can keep the lion's share of the business and beat the competition." To this end, the Corporate Help Desk Solution (CHDS) project was adopted to implement a corporate system that would enhance customer service quality and productivity through preventive and timely resolution of fault incidents, while significantly reducing costs.

A help desk team and plan were developed to identify the problem, define it, determine the requirements, and select and implement a resolution. In their analysis, they came to six major conclusions:

1. Lack of systems integration is perilously affecting help desk efficiency.

□ The ten existing systems used to manage troubles/faults create "electronic islands" and consequently render the process of responding to and fixing customer problems inefficient and unnecessarily complex.

□ Different systems are used to manage the same craftsmen for installation and repair, yet they are incompatible with each other. Table 23-1 maps the systems employed by Atlantic Tel.

□ There is no evidence of these systems' communicating adequately with other critical systems such as billing, order provisioning, work management, etc.

□ Current systems provide for adequate individual tracking of problems, but are seriously deficient in analyzing what went wrong. Correlation of individual problems to other symptoms and problems is inefficient.

2. Lack of training is related to help desk.

□ Inadequate and insufficient training contributes directly and indirectly to shortfalls in reliability and customer satisfaction. This is a two-sided issue involving Atlantic Tel, both internally and with external customers.

Figure 23-1 The Atlantic Tel corporate help desk solution vision

☐ Many trouble calls could be averted if more education were provided to customers.

☐ Craftsmen are not optimally trained at diagnosing and fixing faults.

☐ An inordinately high incidence of repeat failures is related to the training problem.

3. Trouble management is too labor intensive.

☐ Labor intensity is the crux of the help desk issue. Nearly three-quarters of the resource required to address faults/troubles is labor.

☐ There is no real time system to match the supply of labor with demand. This resulted in missed appointments and inefficient scheduling of resources.

☐ A system for tracking individual and generalist skills, productivities, and performances of craftsmen was not in place.

4. Access to repair is too confusing to customers.

☐ Access to Atlantic Tel's repair operations, while improved, lack ideal and achievable procedures.

☐ Fifteen percent of calls to business offices are for repairs; they should be directed to the repair operations initially. This results in unproductive effort at the business office, while customers were angered because they had to start down another path to get their problem addressed.

☐ Transfers of problems to the proper owner are "un-seamless" and create customer frustrations, which, in turn, don't promote customer satisfaction.

5. Customer satisfaction needs improvement.
Based on Atlantic Tel's team performance report, there were several areas requiring attention. These data are presented in Tables 23-2 and 23-3.

6. CHDS planning and strategies are proactive but incomplete.

Atlantic Tel's proactive approach to CHDS was orderly, timely, and intelligent, with proper focus and attention paid to problem definition, needs assessment, and overall project management and planning. Atlantic Tel's vision, goals, and objectives are shown in Table 23-4.

The commitment to methodically address the CHDS issue obviated any superficial and hasty decisions that, because of the impact on company operations, could have been devastating in the long term. "We do not want to automate a bad process," was an appropriate statement by one respondent. Applying customer satisfaction to the team share bonus plan was commendable, and the parameters in the team performance report appeared to cover all the bases regarding customer satisfaction.

An apt metaphor likened Atlantic Tel to a duck—"smoothe on top but paddling hard underneath"—with the rapid change, past and future, required to maintain and enhance the business. Statistically, Atlantic Tel had, and probably continues to have, its share of competitive challenge, because of newer telecommunications companies: 89% of current revenue base was at potential risk, with a 40% reduction in toll rates in three years.

Table 23-1 Atlantic Tel System/function model

Activity	Dept A	Dept B	Dept C	Dept D	Dept E	Dept F	Dept G	Dept H
Incient	D*	I*	I*	I*	I*	Telco	Walk-In	TPM
Logged *From* Analysis, Diagnosis	w/C	S*	w/A	S*	S*	S*	S*	S*
Dispatch *Technician*	Yes	Yes	Yes	Yes	Yes	Yes	Yes	Yes
# Help Desk Systems Used	3	3	1	3	1	2	1	1

*D = Direct; I = Indirect; S = Self

Based on the six major conclusions cited above, the help desk project team made four recommendations:

1. Tighter focus on the real issues is needed.
The help desk project team began to focus and concentrate on some of the major issues emerging from its work to date, which are summarized in Table 23-5. Some of these issues included the following facts:

→ There is a need for seamless and fewer call transfers of trouble reports.

Table 23-2 Customer satisfaction needs improvement

| | | RATING* | |
Category	1992	1993	% Improvement
Repair Service	56%	42%	(14%)
Installation Service	15%	11%	(4%)
Access to Service	63%	63%	0
Operator Service	100%	100%	0
Network Service	94%	99%	5%
Special Service	63%	74%	9%
Total	61%	63%	2%

*Optimum = 100%

Table 23-3 Customer satisfaction needs Improvement

Item	% Successes/Plan
Repeat Trouble Reports	None
Delay Days	None
Customers not served (install)	None
Repair Appointments missed	8%
Due Dates Met—(Int. Svcs)	17%
Installation Appointments missed	20%
00s Cleared < 24 hours (Res.)	33%
00s Cleared < 3 hours (Bus. Data)	33%
Trouble Reports	20%

→ Atlantic Tel needs to further understand and analyze the shortfalls in missed appointments, repeat troubles, late installations, and cost of troubles/faults.

→ Current perceptions need validation.

→ The relationship between reliability, training, and customer satisfaction, including responsiveness, needs to be better understood as this could have significant impact on the project.

→ The project team should have continued to keep others in Atlantic Tel informed of their purpose, progress, and aims, keeping in mind the question, What is in it for me?

In addition, during the definition phase, it would be advantageous to review elements of the project with selected customers to get a feel for their reactions and inputs. A focus group could be a good medium for this.

Table 23-4 Vision and Objectives

Atlantic Tel is committed to maintaining and enhancing its market leadership in service reliability, responsiveness, quality of repairs and customer liaison and satisfaction.

GOALS	MEASURE
Increase Customer Satisfaction	* 98% of customers will rate us good/excellent
	* Single point of contact
Decrease Troubles and Faults	* 10% fewer troubles/year
	* Atlantic Tel detected faults greater than customer detected
	* Ability to measure
	Customer detected faults
	Number of troubles per fault
Decrease Clearing Time	* Meet specific standards 100% of time
	* Response time
Decrease Repeat Reports	* No repeat reports
No Increase in Cost	* Total cost of trouble management to remain consistent with '93 levels from '94 to '97
	* Understand correlation of reliability and cost
Employee Participation/Recognition	* Atlantic Tel employees will be directly involved in creating customer satisfaction

→ The labor component of help desk operation was three-quarters of total cost, and should be examined carefully with respect to productivity and efficiency, and training and skills of craftsmen as well as receptionists, dispatchers and testers.

→ Organizationally, it is evident that further streamlining could have been achieved, which would have helped enhance customer satisfaction as well as improved costs.

→ Consolidation of residential, voice, business voice data, and mobile services repair reception would help the customer simplify the process of logging a problem while eventually helping to reduce staff.

→ In lieu of having several dispatchers and testers for each business unit and each region, a central clearinghouse could handle these functions on a 24 hour a day, 7 day a week basis. Also, it could accelerate the level of technical knowledge and skill to those handling troubles so that fewer call transfers would be required.

2. An audit of all policies, procedures and practices that are relevant to the help desk should be accelerated as a critical element of the project plan.

→ A salient example is the escalation procedure for taking a problem to its next level of expertise, after a prescribed time period.

→ An up-to-date assessment of these rules and guidelines and how they are being followed are essential in understanding and designing the solutions to the trouble and fault management task.

→ Atlantic does not want to automate a process that is either not working or is nonexistent.

3. Customer satisfaction is a perceived phenomenon, and a public relations marketing effort should be considered to convince customers and employees alike, that the commitment for better service is real.

→ A simple, direct mail flier posted in the monthly bill would be nominal effort and expense.

→ The same brochure or flier could be included in employee's pay envelopes.

→ A slogan to capture the intent, objectives and concerns for customer satisfaction should be developed. The theme would be something on the order of "Perfect Service."

4. Logistics and materials should be added to the scope of the help desk project.

There is a definite correlation between spare parts and materials availability and reliability and customer satisfaction.

→ How many repeat calls are the result of not having the proper unit/part on the first call?

→ What is the incidence of dead-on-arrival units/parts, causing delays and repeat calls?

→ How many missed appointments are caused because the parts or materials are not available?

Table 23-5 The real issues

Repeat Troubles	1993 Ave	Goal
Voice	6%	8%
Data	9%	10%
Repair	16%	15%
Appointments Missed	*1993 Avg*	*Goal*
Install	4%	3%
Repair	15%	10%
Customers Awaiting Installation >1993 Average 10 Days		*Goal*
Main	106.8	10
Regrade	2356.9	150

Cost of Trouble/Faults $24 Million
- 73% Labor
- 24% Materials
- 3% Data Prorcessing

24

Help Desk Case Study: Overseas National Broadcasting Company

*T*HIS CASE STUDY IS ABOUT AN OVERSEAS NATIONAL BROAD-
CASTING COMPANY (ONBC), a fictitious name for a government-
owned, national broadcasting company, outside the United
States. The case is presented in the form of the *actual final
report* which was presented to ONBC in response to their need
for guidance in planning their help desk. The principal aspects
of the ONBC Case which make it relevant include:

• The fact that ONBC's information technoloy strategy included a brand new help desk that could actually add value to
the company while improving a rather tarnished image of the
IT group.

• The new help desk was seen by ONBC as the most important medium for user satisfaction.

• Almost every department within ONBC also had its own
individual help desk, because the primary help desk was not
fulfilling user needs.

The excerpts of the Final Report on ONBC's Help Desk study represent a look at then existing situations and what was needed.

Background

The Overseas National Broadcasting Corporation, while owned by the Overseas National Government, operated without political bias and received most of its funding through annual appropriations from the Commonwealth Parliament. The Corporation consisted of major divisions in radio, television, concert music and marketing.

The *Help Desk Management Consulting Project* was commissioned by the Management Information Systems Division, whose mission was to deliver computing systems to the corporation in support of its goals and objectives. The consultant was recognized as a key contributor to substantial improvements in the effectiveness of ONBC, providing its 1100 users with 99.7 percent availability. Figures 24-1 and 24-2 show the ONBC organizational structure.

Methodology

The approach of the Help Desk Management Consulting Project was to gather appropriate information from corporate personnel who were involved in providing user support services as well as those classified as users of the hotline. Information was derived from:

- Personal interviews with staff, usually one-on-one.

- Appropriate documents, such as ONBC management information standards, job descriptions, call reports, procedures and other similar records.

Interviews with staff were aimed at eliciting respondents' attitudes and perceptions in relation to:

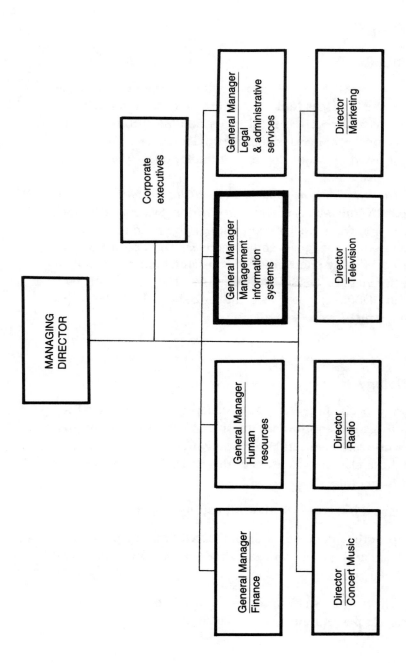

FIGURE 24-1 ONBC's top organizational structure

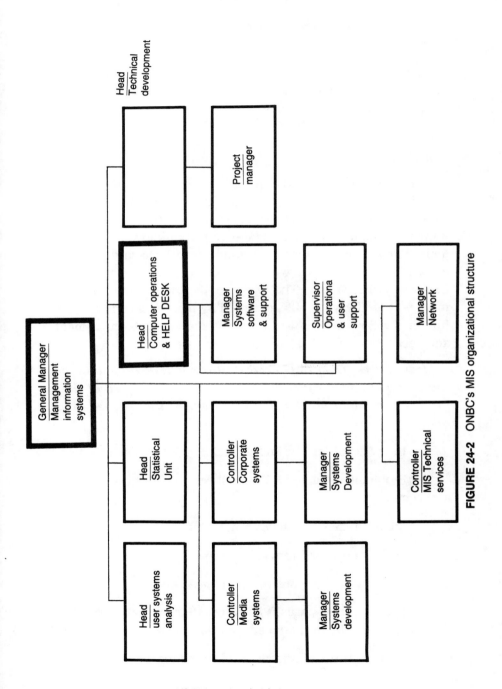

FIGURE 24-2 ONBC's MIS organizational structure

- Positive as well as negative aspects of user support.

- Suggestions for enhancement, expansion and overall commentary.

A brief user survey was conducted and respondents were guaranteed anonymity in an effort to get candid feedback.

Conclusions

Management. A positive image of MIS was developed and significantly enhanced by provision and operation of the user support hotline. Some key issues were resolved: Recent and imminent changes in the hotline involved unknown user problems. Management reports indicating repeat calls and problem escalation, for example, were inadequate. The escalation process was "laissez-faire." The pressure for productivity improvement wasn't always readily accepted by the ONBC unions. The hotline supervisor often received calls directly. Job enrichment and succession planning programs were weak.

Procedures. Operators needed training in dealing with the increasingly wider range and more complex nature of user problems and queries. Some of the problems that needed to be addressed were:

— Users identified the lack of training as a major problem.

— Problems documented on call reports lacked constancy and accuracy.

— Inconstancies prevailed in handling calls.

— Problem ownership was too vague.

— There was little control of forwarded calls.

— A general consensus from respondents was that the Hotline should have been the focal point for all remedial requests.

— There was no prioritization of incoming calls.

— Only one telephone line was specifically reserved for hotline calls.

— The differences in time zones of the ONBC customer bases were not adequately considered.

Several separate call-handling procedures and forms existed in standards, network services, reports, and operations. An indeterminate number of calls bypassed the hotline. A fault symptoms/fix check list was incomplete, but was nevertheless used by hotline operators. Duty statements needed updating. Backup procedures were needed for catastrophic failures.

Training Issues. Training of Hotline operators was too informal and shallow. Training, in general, was decentralized and needed better control. A "skills/knowledge profile" pilot was imminent via business analysis.

User Feedback. Users were generally quite satisfied with the hotline, but broader coverage was suggested. Users perceived significant difference in hotline personnel skill levels.

Small Systems. Only two to three PC calls were logged per week but many were not reported to user support. PC Link and similar tools facilitate the netwok and could have been involved in a network failure.

Call Handling Trends. Over 3,600 calls were taken, annually:

Monthly Average	304
High (August)	414
Low (April)	209
Most calls were user problems:	24%–41%
Other problems	22%–37%
Equipment	15%–32%
Communications	70%–20%
Applications	3%–10%

Most calls occurred between 9:00 a.m. and 10:00 a.m. Heaviest activity occurred during the first 10 days of month, and on Thursdays. Two thirds of calls were handled independently by the hotline. 58 percent of the remaining third involved the computer vendor. 47 percent of calls were not closed. The recorded time to close calls averaged from 0.32 hours to 3.44 hours.

Recommendations

Management

We felt that management should have emphasized a new MIS OPS Mission statement that incorporates a zero call, 100% availability philosophy. We also realized the company needed to:

→ Restructure the user support organization.

→ Utilize administrative assistants as primary call screeners.

→ Install another hotline telephone line; and one line for *incoming* and one for *outgoing* calls.

→ Optimize the user support officers' time—not answering calls but receiving forwarded calls that utilize his knowledge and expertise.

→ Employ dedicated specialists in the areas of news, payroll, and small systems

(These personnel should have been within a moment's reach of the call screener or user support officer, either via beeper or by being physically located adjacent to the hotline. They would not have needed to report organizationally to user support, but could have rotated from their respective organizations in much the same fashion as the operators. During idle periods they could have done their normal work and/or helped develop and continually refine users' trouble-shooting documentation. Eventually, depending on the workload, these positions might have become permanent, which, being newly created job opportunities, would have been beneficial to unions as well as management of ONBC.)

→ Optimize MIS coordinators and, from the outset, instill in them the necessity to report all critical problems/solutions through the hotline.

→ Accommodate 7 × 24 coverage by employing an answering service (live) during off hours and covering all hours with standby personnel reachable immediately by beeper/phone.

Based upon results of this project and other work, management should have specified, selected and implemented an automated call-handling system in order to accomplish these tasks:

— Provide comprehensive management control

— Integrate the SWS system, especially for warranty/service tracking continuity

— Provide management reports including escalation

— Establish performance measurements

— Support WAS coordinators

— Focus on the further development of human relations, via job enrichment/succession planning programs; fail-safe backup procedures to avoid castastrophic failures (initiating plans and strategies to become a more *proactive* organization)

— Publicize positive user feedback, from this and follow-on surveys.

Procedures and Programs

The survey also recommended the following procedural changes;

• Distribute the Hotline "checklist" as a user-friendly troubleshooting guide.

• Consolidate and integrate various existing hotlines.

• Investigate artificial intelligence tools and techniques for developing a library of faults and fixes.

• Implement a regularly scheduled user survey. ("How did we do?").

Training

Among the recommendations, these should be considered:

• Schedule experienced call handlers to work with consultants for news training.

• Dispatch experienced hotline personnel as well as trainees to user field locations to provide and receive instruction, including "hands on" help to users. This would also have had a positive impact on how users perceive MIS and user support.

• Implement training seminar on: product and application familiarity; consistency in providing answers and suggestions; telephone technique; and customer relations.

• Develop the business analysis skills profile program.

• Accelerate training as a top priority.

Mission/Strategies

The mission of the MIS operations department, including the user support group was to help keep the community running and solve any problems or queries that arose. The functions of the organization were largely of an educational nature and involved fiinding other experts to convey answers to the end user. The role was of resource broker and problem/answer intermediary. Users of the hotline, according to the sample in this project, tended to also be intermediaries representing larger end user groups. The mission of the group seemed to be adequately understood both within and outside and there seemed to be a common understanding of what was to be done. The group appeared to work well as a team and a healthy esprit existed.

Strategically, the group seemed very much in a reactive mode. Also, the strategy of rotating part-time computer operators, while working well in the past, needed to be carefully reviewed in light of the much heavier than anticipated workload with new projects such as News, Payroll and others.

Business Controls

The consciousness of the need for control within the ONBC MIS functions was clearly evident at upper and middle management levels. The desire for control existed but in reality the practice of business control clearly fell short of the need. Management was aware of this and was addressing the issue of control within the scope of this and future studies and programs.

Resource Management

While MIS and the hotline have enjoyed an inner positive image, the potential criticalness and unreadiness to address the programs already mentioned could have reversed the excellent perception that was created. Much of the success was a factor of teamwork and matrix management in the sense that the key contributors added value over and above their duty statements.

More structure needed to be incorporated into the system of handling user problems. ONBC management was also aware of this and was pursuing measures to manage this change with a minimum impact on the creative and productive attitudes of its employees.

The implementation of an automated call handling system would have impacted a number of users and providers of User Support and the associated sensitivities of those involved would have been respected.

Performance Metrics

Performance metrics for User Support were inadequate for existing and future demands. Manual data existed but was not used to generate meaningful management information control.

An automated system should have been selected and implemented in Phases Two and Three which could have addressed this need.

A sample of the critical performance measures included:

— Number of calls, by: priority, problem type, source, time of day/month.

— Call closure: % of total, response times.

— Disposition of calls: ONBC, Vendors.

— Operator efficiency.

— User Feedback: ratings, suggestions.

User Satisfaction

The level of user satisfaction with User Support and the hotline was quite positive. Included in the recommendations of this report was a suggestion to contact users on a regular basis, in person and through ONBC's newsletter. Because of logistics problems, the internal user satisfaction questionnaire, planned as part of this study, was deferred and was to be conducted by ONBC using a later edition of the newsletter as the instrument.

Hotline Call Analysis

The hotline call analysis included in the following pages describes in detail the call activity of two complete months of activity, chosen at random. While the data was not statistically absolutely errorless, qualitative tests suggest that the resultant figures were representative.

The following tables provide useful data and recommendations for the fast-growing field of management assistance to users and suppliers of computers and related products and service.

Table 24-1 Users Gave the Hotline Some High Marks

Hotline Characteristics	Scores		
	Average	High	Low
Courtesy/Attitude	1.5	1	2
Follow-Up	1.5	1	2
Responsiveness	1.6	1	3
	1.9	1	4
Ability to Help	2.1	1	3
Overall Timeliness	2.3	1	4
Knowledge of Operators	2.9	2	5

Score Values:
1 = Excellent, 5
= Unacceptable

Table 24-2 Hotline Call Analysis with Suggestions For Improvement

- **Message/answering service (system down status)**
- **Prioritize users' needs**
- **Issue troubleshooting manuals**
- **Improve consistency of answers to problems**
- **Be more PC responsive**
- **General help (hand holding)**
- **On-the-job training**
- **Wider coverage (7 × 24)**

Table 24-3 Random Comments

"Quality of hotline depends on who you strike"
"Quite happy"
"I'll fumble around—my last resort is the hotline"
"Pretty good"
"Often times I know the (hotline's) remedies were not correct—'On/Off' for example"
"Needs more training"
"Pretty helpful"

Table 24-4 Hotline Trouble-Shooting Menu

TERMINAL FAULTS
No Power to Terminal
Power But No Response
No Response Only To
    One User
No Response To All
    Terminals On Floor
Terminal Hung Half Way
    Through Interact.
    Session.
Strange Characters On
    Screen
All Keystrokes Appear On
    Attached Printer
No Response From
    System—Keystrokes
    on Screen
Receiving Messages When
    Connecting From
    LOCAL
Session Limit Reached
Insufficient Node
    Resources
Service XXXX Not Known
Service XXXX Not
    Available
User Authorization Failure

PRINTER FAULTS
Dump Printers
Queued Printers
Job Queued To Printer But
    Nothing Printing
Job Queued to Printer &
    Error Message
    Received
Job on Printer in
    Hyroglyphics

APPLICATION FAULTS

GENERAL ENQUIRIES
All-in-1 Enquiries
Errors Encountered Within
    All-in-1
Only Part Of The
    Document Prints
Personal Computers (PC's)
Access To Applications
New Passwords Or Reset
    Passwords
Increase Disk Quota

CHECKING & TESTING
COMMUNICATION EQUIPMENT
Using Terminal Server
    Manager (TSM)
MICOM—Micro Data
    Concentrator
DecServer 100/200
Swapping A DecServer
    100/200
DecSa Ethernet Terminal
    Server
De-Mux and MuxServer
DecMux and MuxServer
    Introduction
Basic Configuration Of A
    MuxServer to
    DecMux/s
Connecting A MuxServer to
    DecMux/s
Mapping The MuxServer to
    DecMux/s
Connecting to Dec/Mux/s
Bit Synchronous
    Processor (BSP)

Table 24-5 Hotline User Survey

1. How many times within the past 12 months did you use the hotline?
2. How many times within the *next* 12 months do you think you'll use the hotline?
3. On a scale of 1 to 5, where 1 is excellent and 5 is poor, please rate the following from your hotline experience(s):
   - A. Responsiveness of hotline attendants:
   - B. Courtesy/attitude of hotline attendants:
   - C. Expertise of hotline attendants:
   - D. Quality of service from hotline attendants:
   - E. Speed of addressing and fixing your problems:
   - F. Follow-up:
4. Please write any comments you have about the hotline (such as strengths and weaknessess, for example);
5. What are your suggestions for improving the hotline?

25

Help Desk Case Study: ComCorp

Managing operations in a smaller company

*T*HIS CASE STUDY IS ABOUT COMCORP, A FICTITIOUS NAME for a manufacturer of communications equipment. The case is presented as an example of a smaller service organization's philosophy and strategy for managing their help desk.

The principal aspects about the ComCorp Case, which make it relevant, include:

The interesting approach to managing a smaller operation's help desk, which covered several different functions, including:

—Calls from customers reporting trouble or asking questions.

—Calls from self maintenance customers reporting trouble or asking questions about equipment coming in or being shipped from the repair center.

—Calls from field engineers asking questions about a specific problem or site they were working on, and/or escalating problems.

— The help desk's importance in attaining customer satisfaction.

— The employment of a simple customer survey to stay in touch with customers.

— The escalation process and employment of help desk resources.

Background

The ComCorp help desk supported four hundred customers of communications equipment and 10 field engineers who called the help desk for further assistance or to close a call. About twenty-five calls a day were taken, of which only 4 or 5 required on site service. The bulk of calls were closed during the initial contact by the customer. It operated with a "live" dispatcher from 8 to 5, Mondays through Fridays, excluding holidays. From 5 to 8 in the evening, a field engineer was on duty. All other times were covered by an answering machine. ComCorp used this system to tout 24-hour coverage, 7 days a week. Figure 25-1 shows the call flow and escalation process, with available resources.

What Worked Well at the ComCorp Help Desk

Features of the ComCorp help desk that proved to be effective included:

▶ *Diagnostics* Fortunately, ComCorp products were fairly simple and had comprehensive diagnostics built into them. On a few occasions, the director of technical support was able to intervene from his monitor in New Jersey, to handle a network problem involving nodes in the United Kingdom, France and Houston, Texas.

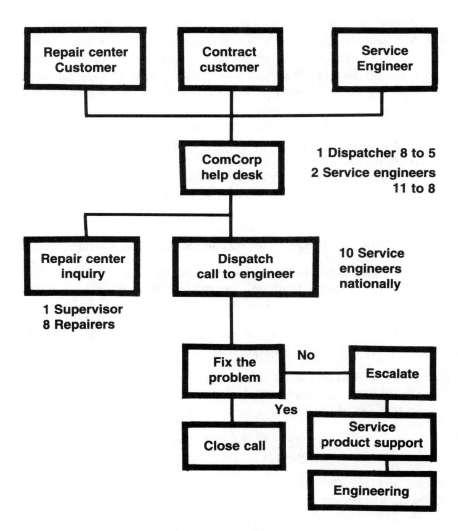

Figure 25-1 Algorithm of Call Flow and Resources

► *Dispatcher.* The dispatcher was a pleasant young lady who never got rattled, despite the pressures of being the sole person to answer the help desk telephone. If another customer or engineer placed a call while she was already engaged, they were bounced directly to one of the two service engineers on duty. Customers got to know her voice and truly identified her with the entire company when they called in. Service engineers did the same even though few of the customers and remote service engineers ever met the dispatcher, personally. Having a single operator had the advantage of providing very *personal* service, and a great rapport was developed. Of course, when she was absent because of vacation or illness, a substitute took over and the operation was sometimes noticeably and negatively affected.

Other advantages with this single focal point were:

► The fact that, over time, she became adept in analyzing faults and could actually tell the caller how to fix the problem in many situations. Her knowledge expanded dramatically.

► Her attitude was great and she loved interacting and helping customers whom she grew to know over several years.

► While not a technical expert, the dispatcher became well versed in the products and their faults. But she was paid a salary which was equivalent to a middle range secretary's salary.

► She was a good call screener and worked well with the service engineers on duty.

► *Help Desk Service Engineers.* Two service engineers were always on hand so that, if the dispatcher couldn't close the call herself, she had technical backup, at her side—literally. These service engineers were assigned to the help desk on a rotational basis, in one-month shifts. When they were not engaged with customer or other field problems, they were able to study new product maintenance features and enchance their service skills.

► *Customer Satisfaction Survey.* A simple post card type of customer survey with five easy questions were initiated. This

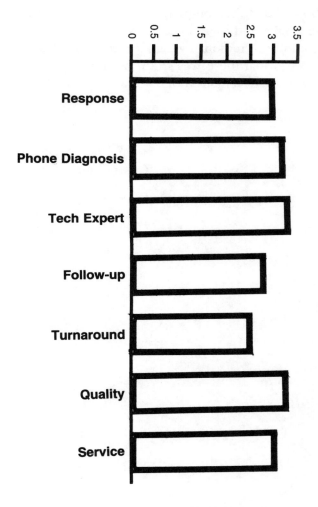

Figure 25-2
ComCorp Customer Satisfaction
Survey (4=High; 1=Low)

survey had the effect of enhancing the bonding with customers because it showed that the company was interested in them. A sample of the results of the survey is shown in Figure 25-2. The level of satisfaction was reasonably high for all factors. However, the survey showed that there was still room for improvement. Here is a valuable management tool.

SECTION

VI

Appendices

Appendix

A

Model for Selecting Help Desk Software

*T*HE SELECTION OF THE RIGHT HELP DESK SOFTWARE IS contingent on establishing functional specifications that support the business needs of the specific help desk to be planned or improved. It therefore is necessary to determine the business needs, identify potential software systems, and conduct a comprehensive evaluation to match needs with capabilities. Most information used in the evaluation can be obtained through system demonstrations and vendor interviews with a "short list" of potential help desk software systems developers.

Additionally, a visit to potential vendors' *users* to view Help Desk software in actual use is recommended. An in-house pilot test can serve as an audit to assure that the help desk software system is sufficient for current and future needs.

The Selection Index (SI) helps rank the final system candidates, and is expressed as:

*SI = RF * WF*
SI = Selection Index
RF = Rating Factor: 10 is best and 1 is worst, in terms of meeting the needs of the help desk in question

WF = Weight Factor, which provides a weight to the individual attributes (See Table AA-1)

The Selection Index (SI) helps prioritize the *attributes* of the help desk software system. Of course, a very important factor in addition to the SI is the *cost* of the help desk system and support.

Table AA-1 Selection model for obtaining help desk software

Attribute	Weight	Rating Factor	Selection Index	Maximum Score
Call Handling	15	6	90	150
Dispatching	10	4	40	100
Technical Assistance	15	5	75	150
Warranty Management	5	6	30	50
Contract Management	5	7	35	50
Revision/Configuration Control	5	8	40	50
Inventory Control	5	7	35	50
Spare Parts Order Processing	5	7	35	50
Depot Management	5	7	35	50
Hot Line	35	9	315	350
Escalation Procedures	25	8	200	250
Training	15	6	90	150
User Friendliness	10	3	30	100
User Interface	10	6	60	100
Report Generator	10	6	60	100
Update Management	8	6	48	80
Security	8	7	56	80
Maintenance	8	7	56	80
Hardware Compatibility	6	8	48	60
Software Compatibility	6	8	48	60
User Visits	50	6	300	500
Pilot Test	100	8	800	1000
Vendor Profile*	40	5	200	400

* = Financial Condition, Active User Group and Attitude

B

Sample Help Desk Consulting Proposal

*T*HE FOLLOWING IS FROM AN ACTUAL WINNING PROPOSAL for help desk consulting. Identities of the companies involved have been disguised. This particular proposal was offered on a project basis.

Introduction

Enterprise welcomes the opportunity to present this consulting project overview to Emu Industries (EMU). The project as defined here has developed out of discussions between EMU and Enterprise over recent months. Enterprise has a proven record in regard to its own service activities and with this background has provided consulting to many of its customers who have similar service requirements.

EMU, as with most high technology service businesses, has experienced changing technological trends in the communications marketplace and has recognized how these have increasingly impacted their operating efficiency and customer satisfaction.

This solution from Enterprise addresses the interest expressed by EMU around user support systems (help desks) and service management systems. It will describe our recommended approach to conduct a help desk system solution and implementation project for the EMU network management center.

Help Desk System Project Overview

The help desk project, developed and managed by Enterprise, provides consulting to EMU to objectively address the operational and support systems requirements of the network management center. Enterprise's consultants will appraise all aspects of existing operations to define the existing process, policies, and procedures. This information will be analyzed, validating and specifying the requirements for the Help Desk against those already defined.

The resultant functional requirement will be matched to a most appropriate packaged solution, and Enterprise will propose a full implementation plan for the entire project to be installed on existing Enterprise systems.

The help desk system project, developed and managed utilizing Enterprise's proprietary Enterprise Project Maker Technique (PMT), provides consulting and senior project implementation resources to EMU to objectively address the operational and developing needs of its organization. This technique will ensure that the proposed solution is delivered on time and within budget.

Background

EMU has recognized that a critical factor in the application of new technology is service. In today's deregulated environment, pressures have been brought to bear upon the utilization of technology to provide a quality service to users while maintaining a focus on cost control and efficiency of operations.

EMU's network management center has been meeting the basic requirement for a user support system, primarily via a manual process, and wishes to apply the developing technologies of Enterprise's service expertise to automate this process. To do this it must better understand its current position and potential exposure to a rapidly changing technical, business, and human resource environment. Applying this process means EMU will ensure both internal and external customer satisfaction, and maintain its competitive advantage.

Enterprise Computer Corporation, itself a major user of system-based user support technologies, has experienced the same situations in meeting the challenges of growth and new development. Enterprise provides such services as a line of business with the objectives of high availability, managed costs, and customer satisfaction as paramount. In order to provide profitable service in an increasingly competitive environment while meeting customer requirements, Enterprise had to develop a better understanding of how it should manage and improve upon a quality level of service.

It is this experience Enterprise brings to EMU. Enterprise makes available the support management expertise developed over the past nine years and the expertise of thousands of staff from its worldwide support organization. Enterprise believes that EMU could benefit greatly by sharing in the wealth of expertise accumulated in the specific service areas described in this document.

Project Scope

Enterprise has spent time with EMU reviewing the perceived requirements for an operational support system in order to develop an understanding of the scope of their needs. This has resulted in this fall proposal document, defining how Enterprise will go about designing the solution and its ensuing implementation project plan.

A successful project is one that produces deliverables on time, according to specification and agreed quality, and within budget as committed to during the project. This success is dependent upon careful planning and preparation, as this forms the foundation upon which the latter stages of the implementation are built. Enterprise uses PMT to carefully plan and prepare in the early phases so that content and detail required in the latter phases is consistent with, and built upon, data collected during the earlier phases.

It is an integral part of the technique that at the completion of each phase, the customer has agreed to the outputs/deliverables with the prime contractor, including the cost and time frame required to successfully complete the next phase. Any requested changes to agreed documents such as the requirements specification or the functional specification will be incorporated into the project through a change control mechanism.

To achieve the project deliverable in the shortest possible time frame, Enterprise will combine several phases, delivering the entire project in two phases. This will have the added advantage of making each individual phase a value-added project in itself. This means that if EMU does not wish to take advantage of Enterprise's Phase Two recommendation, EMU's investment in Phase One will be in itself a valuable project document.

Phase One

Enterprise will develop an initial appraisal of EMU's existing help desk operations and its interaction with the four operating companies and other major customers. All information required to develop the designated requirement will be gathered. From this information a base line is established, clearly defining where EMU help desk operations are within the exiting environment. This is essential for the successful completion of the project and will allow for accurate design of the solution.

EMU believes most of the information required already exists, which should minimize the time required to complete this task. If so, definition can be completed in ten working days. Any sub-projects that may be required would be defined and scoped at this time.

A detailed analysis of the data collected in the early phase will validate EMU's requirements. From these requirements Enterprise's consultants will establish the project plan and the proposed functionality. These requirements will be validated with EMU prior to proceeding.

The functional requirements will be produced, including the acceptance testing requirements that Enterprise, as prime contractor, will deliver. Enterprise will specify the design of the solution components that will be packaged for EMU's requirements.

A project implementation plan will be developed. The entire output of Phase One will be compiled in a document, complete with pricing for the package and implementation project for Phase Two.

It is estimated that this could be delivered in twenty working days from the date of authorization. The price of Phase One is $30,175. Refer to the section on project pricing for complete pricing details.

Phase Two

Phase Two comprises implementation and installation as proposed in Phase One, including all solution components, acceptance testing, facilities preparations, training, and documentations. An assessment of achievement and review of operations following acceptance testing will take place. Any future requirement will be evaluated to achieve new or changed goals.

Project Objectives

Upon acceptance of this proposal, Enterprise will prepare a list of the operational data, financial and managerial reports, policies, and procedures required to commence Phase One of the project. Once this information is gathered, the project will be ready to enter Phase One. If pertinent information is not available a joint decision will be reached upon its effect on the proposed project.

A key component of Phase One is the performance of an assessment of existing operations, or, in other words, establishing a base line. This is essentially an information collection, compilation, and assessment phase. This will involve the historical and current information requested, as well as detailed on-site analysis of information extracted from structured interviews with key EMU staff.

The data will, in most cases, be available from current management information systems and reports, policy and procedures manuals, and organizational instructional documents which have developed to form the basis of existing operations. In cases where pertinent data does not exist, or, for some reason, may not be available to Enterprise, it is requested that the appropriate individual within EMU facilitate the effort to develop or obtain the information or a suitable subset of it.

Initially, an Enterprise project manager will bring together a team of EMU personnel for a project help desk familiarization. Together with the Enterprise consultants they will review the requested data generated and hold a project start-up meeting. This meeting serves as an introduction of the project personnel to the EMU management team, establishes management participation in the project, and establishes desired communicaion linkages. It also includes the specification of milestones and deliverables. It is important that there be significant interaction and feedback to the consulting team, highlighting areas of concern and sensitivity.   Some of the tasks and activities of the project team will occur away from EMU premises.

The total activities of the project will comprise:

• Current Position Assessment (includes a review of existing operations, goals and objectives, measurement of performance against objectives, and measurement of operational needs)

• Tools in use and existing processes

• Capacity and capability to support operations (human resource utilization)

• Management and reporting

From an in-depth assessment of the help desk function, focusing on the areas of operations that impact EMU needs, Enterprise will develop a requirements analysis. The help desk's business components will be addressed by evaluating the current processes in place, identifying issues and needs, and defining the impact of known future plans on current operations, problem call handling and escalation, service level definition, human resource development, network requirements, measurement, management, and reporting.

An analysis of help desk requirements will be developed into a functional specification. It will define terminology, specify sections of operational requirements, define environmental requirements, quality requirements, documentation requirements, training requirements, and the change in management process, and it will specify other unique requirements.

Valuable output from the consultants' activities will be included in an operational assessment report, with recommendations focused on attaining EMU's business objectives for the help desk function. The content of this report will include:

— An assessment of the current situation

— Recommendations for improved operations

— An assessment of risks to current and future help desk operations, and the needs and issues facing the operation

— Recommendations for operational reporting requirements

— Recommendations for operational measurements

— Recommendations for other help desk tools as observed

— Recommendatons for the cost effective operations in the context of current business and known future plans

— Sample reports, graphs, empirical supporting data where applicable and available

Enterprise will also deliver to EMU the acceptance criteria for the recommended solution. The solution plan, including a fully priced implementation and installation plan, will be presented along with the consultants' findings and recommendations.

Phase Two activities are summarized in the following list:

1. Sign contracts with third parties if applicable

2. Plan delivery of solution

.3. Prepare acceptance test

4. Test solution

5. Prepare site requirements

6. Test for change management and prepare for solution introduction

7. Manage, deliver, and install solution

8. Prepare customers for change

9. Train users

10. Prepare documentation

11. Perform acceptance testing

12. Finalize documentation

13. Facilitate introduction

14. Review project

15. Provide warranty and/or contract support

16. Review further requirements

Project Assumptions

This proposal is based on a number of basic assumptions: EMU's management desires to understand and improve its current methods and level of service for its network management centers' help desks; EMU will appoint a Project Interface Representative (PIR), who will assume the responsibility for the managerial decisions affecting the project and who will provide the necessary authority for Enterprise employees to gain access to required information; Enterprise will appoint a project manager, responsible to the PIR, working in conjunction with project managers or staff detailed by EMU for the life of the project;

EMU's management and key employees will actively participate and cooperate with the project effort; EMU's current organizational structure will be in place throughout the project and for one year thereafter; EMU will provide the consulting team with the information/data necessary to successfully complete the project; EMU will provide reasonable access and suitable workspace within each major office/facility. This should consist of secure cabinets, rooms for confidential meetings, and a workspace with communications capability; EMU's management will alert the consulting team to areas of sensitivity with regard to employees issues (individual or organization), specific confidentiality requirements, and safety and hazardous materials issues.

Project Timetable

Phase One of the project is divided into two parts. The first part will commence as soon as possible after EMU has made available the initial information requested by Enterprise. It is estimated that this task can be completed within ten working days.

The second part of Phase One will follow immediately and should be completed in twenty working days. At the completion, a report will be presented, which will provide functional requirements, system design specification, acceptance test specification, and the project implementation plan. It may be necessary to include a break period during this phase to allow for the scheduling and travel requirements of Enterprise consultants or third party staff.

Phase Two duration cannot yet be defined and will be included as an output from Phase One.

Project Pricing

The price for Phase One is $30,175 in professional fees, plus additional expenses, as incurred. A full breakdown of the enclosed activities follows and is estimated at $4,670. These expenses will be managed within 10% or application will be made to the PIR for approval prior to assumption of the expense.

Phase Two pricing will be provided as an output of Phase One. Enterprise has proceeded with this proposal on the knowledge that EMU had initially suggested a cost for the software package of approximately $100,000.

Estimated Expenses include:

Accommodations per day: $150
Per diem: $80
Airfare: $1500

Additional expenses are on a reimbursable basis, billable upon completion of each project phase. These will only be incurred for travel and accommodation outside of the Springfield Metropolitan Area.

Business Practices

The consulting team will not publish, distribute, sell, or make known any confidential or proprietary information supplied by EMU, unless specifically authorized to do so in writing. The consulting team will alert EMU and Enterprise to any potential areas of conflict of interest. Also, the consulting team will alert EMU's management to an unforeseen deviations to the proposed schedule.

All proprietary work results will become the sole property of EMU. It should also be understood that as employees of Enterprise Computer Corporation, the consulting team cannot divulge, sell, or share Enterprise's proprietary or confidential systems, processes, or information. However, experiences gained in implementaton of these and other systems may be part of the information behind the project. Similarly, the confidentiality requirements of EMU will be honored by the project team.

Appendix

C

Model for Measuring Help Desk Productivity

*T*HE FOLLOWING IS ONE METHOD OF MEASURING HELP DESK PRODUCTIVITY. It is not without flaws, but it at least puts a stake in the ground for attempting to measure help desk productivity:

$$[(u2 \div s2) \times (c2 \div mttcc2) \times I2] \div [(u1 \div s1) \times (c1 \div mttcc1) \times I1]$$

Where:

u2 =	*Average number of users over time period 2*
s2 =	*Average number of staff over time period 2*
c2 =	*Average number of calls per day over time period 2*
mttcc2 =	*Mean time to close call successfully over time period 2*
I2 =	*Average index of user or customer satisfaction over time period 2*

Where: *1 = Poor*
               2 = Fair

$3 = Good$

$4 = Excellent$

And:

$u1 =$ *Average number of users over time period 1*

$s1 =$ *Average number of staff over time period 1*

$c1 =$ *Average number of calls per day over time period 1*

$mttcc1 =$ *Mean time to close call successfully over time period 1*

$I1 =$ *Average index of user of customer satisfaction over time period 1*

Where: *1 = Poor*

          2 = Fair

          3 = Good

          4 = Excellent

And:

Where Time Period 1 occurs before Time Period 2

For example:

Frenetic Software, Inc., desiring to enhance its help desk in 1993, handled about 356 calls per day with a staff of 13. The average time to close calls (MTTCC) was 32 minutes. Frenetic's help desk served 1,234 users, who collectively gave Frenetic a Fair (2) rating in terms of user satisfaction.

A year later, following a concerted effort to improve its services, Frenetic took an average of 487 calls per day from 2,150 users, who rated user satisfaction Good (3). Frenetic now closed calls in 24 minutes. The staff increased to 17.

Calculating productivity, the following equation was solved:

$$[(2150 \div 17) \times (487 \div 24) \times 3] \div [(1234 \div 13) \times (356 \div 32) \times 2] = 3.65$$

or a gain in Productivity of 265%. Not bad!

Furthermore, from these statistics it can be seen that in 1994, 116,880 calls were made to the help desk. By reducing the MTTCC from 32 minutes to 24 minutes (a savings of 8 minutes), through a focused effort to do so, a time savings of 15,584 minutes, or 7.5 man years, is achieved.

Of course, this attempt at quantitatively defining productivity does not take into account all the indirect or "soft" efficiencies in a new or improved help desk. Qualitatively, there are a number of attributes that can be included among "soft" productivities associated with help desks, such as: customer satisfaction, credibility, faster response times, more controlled responses, improved user effectiveness, improved control of assets, reduction of paperwork, more product sales, decreased user stress, and job security.

D

Sample Help Desk Offerings

W ITHIN THIS APPENDIX, LCM1 WILL REFER to Large Computer Manufacturer 1. LCM2 will refer to Large Computer Manufacturer 2. LCM3 will refer to Large Computer Manufacturer 3.

LCM1

This document is intended to briefly describe why LCM1 is a key player in the help desk market, the various components of LCM1's help desk services, and some customer examples of how LCM1 has assisted other companies.

LCM1 can help you:

→ Improve your organization's responsiveness to the needs of your customer (internal or external)

→ Redefine or enhance internal processes and systems to support improved customer service

→ Improve your organization's support to its internal service delivery personnel

→ Help manage costs and/or improve profitability of a service operation

→ Improve overall market share through enhanced customer satisfaction

LCM1's Experience

Why is LCM1 considered a help desk service expert? LCM1 has been in the business of providing help desk services for many years, supporting all our own customers and supporting our employees. This is part of LCM1's CORE business.

In support of customers, LCM1 currently manages fourteen customer support centers located around the world. The need for all fourteen centers is based on specific products developed/supported, geographical considerations, and/or language and cultural differences. In total, LCM1 has invested more than $2 billion to make these centers effective, efficient, and responsive. Furthermore, LCM1's customer support centers are currently supporting hundreds of thousands of customers—globally.

A sample of the customer support center statistics are given in Table AD-1.

Table AD-1 Customer support center statistics

	1981	1991
Call Volume	100,000	3,000,000
Head Count	300	1,700
Customer Satisfaction	7.3	8.6 (maximum is 10)
Employee Turnover	6%	> 2%

Customer support centers handle in excess of 3 million calls annually. According to our latest customer satisfaction survey, LCM1 is clearly responsive. LCM1's customers rated them 8.6 out of a possible 10. Note that these statistics represent an increase in call volume by a factor of 30, an increase in staff by a factor of only 6, an increase in customer satisfaction of 18%, and staff turnover was reduced by over 4%.

LCM1 has over 35 years of accumulated knowledge and experience, which forms the basis for their help desk model, operations, and strategy. This has been developed as a CORE competency within LCM1.

Service Overview

LCM1 defines a help desk as a system, a person, or a group of people that provides a single point of contact and is typically the first level of support for answering "questions" and resolving "problems" from users within a specific organization, a company, or group of companies. More complex or technical questions or problems are managed and escalated by the help desk to the appropriate person, organization, or other contracted third party service providers for resolution. A help desk is a transport and control mechanism between a business problem and its resolution.

LCM1's help desk services are not a "point" or "packaged" product but an enhanced customized service offering. LCM1's motto, "Help Your Information Technology Work" works by transferring LCM1's experience and knowledge to your business. Their help desk service allows you access to the best technology and technical staff, so you can focus on your core business. LCM1 offers help desk support, from the desktop to the data center, in today's open, networked, multivendor environment. And LCM1's help desk service is modular and customized and aims at solving your business problem, not just providing database history or technical advice.

Service Description

Help desk service from LCM1 is a customized response to a strategic business need. It is a valuable service for customers who currently use or wish to implement a single point of contact to provide user information or technical assistance on a specific area of business or technical operations. This information or assistance can be applied to the customer's internal operations or to support and services on their products and services to their own customers.

Help desk service is appropriate for customers who currently use or wish to implement a centralized function (help desk) to provide user information or technical assistance for specific products or services. Help desk service provides implementation of a new help desk, improvement in the effectiveness of an existing help desk operation, or, when appropriate, consolidation of multiple operations. A modular set of services enables customers to obtain assistance in defining the most appropriate architecture for the help desk and implementation and maintenance support in the following areas: call response systems and processes; call management (problem resolution techniques and productivity systems); establishing and monitoring levels of support delivered to users (establishing measurements for customer satisfaction).

The components of LCM1's help desk service are:

→ Help desk consulting (evaluations and assessments)

→ Solution design (new, upgrades, or consolidations) implementation and operations (systems, people, and applications/tools)

→ After-hours coverage

→ Incremental staffing (on-site or remotely)

→ Training (mentoring, development, and delivery)

→ Management, operations, and administration

It is highly recommended that a help desk solution always be preceded by a consulting effort, to ensure that the help desk solution represents the best answer to the customer's business need.

Help Desk Service Features/Benefits

A help desk will allow LCM1's customer to focus more of their resources toward their primary business and/or strategic operations; improve overall market share through enhanced customer satisfaction; offer greater flexibility and responsiveness to increasing numbers of users and new technologies.

Some of the features and benefits a customer will realize when his help desk is providing maximum customer support while improving the profitability of the service operation are shown in Table AD-2.

There are three basic types of delivery scenarios for help desks. These scenarios are based on the perceived environment that the Help Desks will be implemented in. They are:

1. Vendor (LCM1 managed)
2. Shared (LCM1/Client managed)
3. Self (Client managed)

Subgroups of these environments are based upon resource ownership and placement and the types of communication between end user and LCM1. Descriptions of these groups and subgroups are given below.

Table AD-2 Features and benefits of an optimal help desk

Feature	Benefit
Efficiency of call handlings and increased management	Reduced cost and customer satisfaction
Clear process of call escalation and management reporting	Simplicity and efficiency
More appropriate use of technical skills	Greater return on technical investments
Evaluation and planning	Integrated multi-vendor solution
Consulting	Improved support staff performance
Customized design	Optimized operations
Management reporting Single point of contact for systems support and network management	Improved control and increased efficiency and user satisfaction
Access to technical skills	Faster problem resolution
Flexible multi-vendor service	Keeping pace with increased number of new technologies

Vendor (LCM1 managed). The implementation of this option is a complete operation, fully staffed and managed by LCM1. LCM1 will supply all applications/tools and manpower requirements to support and manage a help desk for the client. The intent is that the end user would call a central number and talk to a LCM1 employee, who would perform all responsible functions of the help desk. The LCM1 resources can be resident on the client's site or located remotely on an LCM1 site.

Shared (LCM1/Client managed). The implementation of this option is a "shared" help desk. The responsibilities of LCM1 would be defined based on the needs of the client and the role that the client intended to play in the planning, staffing, and management of the operation.

Typically, LCM1 can supply:

→ Planning and design support (consulting)

→ Implementation support

→ Policy and procedure development

→ Training design and delivery

→ After-hours coverage

→ Incremental staff/technical resources

→ Tools/application selection and implementation

Self (Client managed). The implementation of this help desk scenario is based upon the client's complete ownership and management of their help desk. LCM1 involvement would be in the planning and design phases of the solution.

Delivery Planning and Management

As the first step in a help desk project, either directly on the customer's site or from a remote LCM1 facility, an individual (usually the consultant) determines, with the customer, what the organization's needs and requirements are for a help desk. As part of the definition process, certain information must be acquired by the customer and LCM1. At minimum, the consultant must understand in detail the following:

→ The customer's line of business

→ The customer's market

→ The customer's user base

→ The current problem management process: is the customer setting up a new help desk operation, consolidating multiple help desks, or attempting to improve existing help desk(s) operations?

→ Current and projected call volumes

→ Current call flows and customer's expectations of the "ideal" call flow and/or level of service required

→ Current, if any, applications, tools and tool interfaces (i.e., call/problem management) or what tool interfaces are/will be required

→ Whether help desk will reside on customer's site or remote

→ The customer's operations/administration process and procedures: Does LCM1 provide a standard service offering that would meet the client's needs?

→ The financial/operational overview (i.e., customer's service/maintenance budget, total operations budget, projected budgets/costs, head count, etc.)

→ How the customer is organized and who has the key responsibility for each segment of the organization (including, through discussions with the account team, the customer's political environment)

→ Client's current employee positioning (e.g., career pathing, skills level, turnover, etc.)

→ Key business indicators and metrics, who uses them, and how they are used.

→ What the customer's existing services are and what the customer's needs and requirements for service are

→ How the present vendors are performing

→ What vendor contracts are in place, including expiration dates

→ What types of equipment are presently in use by the customer

→ What the customer's future plans for hardware/software and services are

→ Hardware and software currently used by the customer

→ Network topographies (data and/or voice)

→ Location and size of client's end user base

→ Operational procedures used by customer and vendors

→ Administrative procedures used by the customer

→ Non-contracted EDP and non-EDP service purchased by the customer on per-call or incident occurrence basis

→ Disaster recovery plans

→ Security issues/concerns

Once this evaluation is completed, the level of service and help desk deliverables can be identified, verified with the LCM1 service delivery organization, and proposed.

Implementation/Operations Management

The major components needed to create a help desk include the following:

→ Audit and appraisal of the customer's service needs and help desk requirements (also needed are an understanding of budget restrictions and service delivery capability)

→ Planning and development of the help desk implementation plan

→ Execution of the implementation plan

→ Operations and ongoing management of the help desk

→ Reporting of metrics required to optimize help desk service and service delivery costs and level of service

LCM2's Help Desk Service

LCM2's help desk service provides assistance for multi-vendor personal computer hardware, software, and networks, to dramatically increase the productivity of your computer users. LCM2 response center help desk engineers work directly with your users to assist in PC usage and problem resolution. Service is customized to cover your specific product support needs.

Most user calls are resolved within a few minutes with a single telephone call to the help desk. In the event that on-site or backup assistancce is required, the help desk will obtain additional resources. For example, the help desk may invoke additional support services from LCM2, refer the problem to an appropriate support resource within your organization, or refer the problem to another party that you designate.

Benefits to you include:

Comprehensive support. User assistance encompasses all aspects of your complex hardware, software, and network environment.

Tailored delivery. Supported products are defined by you to focus on the specific multi-vendor hardware and software needs of your users.

Easy access. Users call a single, toll-free number for a direct connection to an expert help desk engineer.

Increased user productivity. LCM2 enhances efficiency by providing expert assistance and resolving most user problems within minutes.

Enhanced decision making. Monthly reports on help desk performance and activity enable you to make informed decisions regarding management of your continuously evolving computer environment.

Service Features include tailored product selection, usage assistance, installation assistance, fault isolation, problem resolution, problem management, and business hour coverage.

Table AD-3 includes descriptions of these features:

LCM3's Help Desk Services: Problem Management Productivity Services
LCM3 problem management productivity services gives you the support you need to make your help desk more effective, while you save on the cost of support. This exclusive LCM3 Service Plan offering gives you the technology and services you need to automate your problem management process. You get proprietary software, access to expert systems, electronic linkages to LCM3 problem response systems, and more. Whether you're logging in problems, looking for the cause of a failure, or closing a problem record, problem management productivity services can help you do it faster and easier.

Access Information More Easily

Using a proprietary software package, problem management productivity services makes problem solving faster and easier from the moment a call is received. No more handwriting or keying in user information to open a problem record—just enter the user's identification, and a pre-filled screen appears. The screens can be custom tailored to meet your specific requirements, providing all the information you need. So a user's name, location, telephone number, equipment, and problem history are all there, pulled from a database LCM3 helps you build.

Improve Your Level of Service

With problem management productivity services, every help desk operator is better equipped to offer the support services your users demand. That's because problem management productivity services is easy to learn and use. Menus let operators choose from a range of options. Predefined screens prompt a request for the information needed to isolate the source of a problem. In addition, problem management productivity services accomplishes many tasks with a single keystroke. That adds up to less time for data collection.

Table AD-3 Service features

Feature   *Delivery Specifications*

TAILORED PRODUCT   Supported products are defined by you and LCM3 to specifically address the support needs of your users. LCM3 engineers have a high level of support experience with a large number of multi-vendor hardware, software, and network products. In addition, LCM3 keeps pace with new multi-vendor products and can support additional applications as customer needs require.

USAGE ASSISTANCE   Help desk engineers provide practical, how-to advice, primarily focused on product functionality, configuration, and documented features. They recommend training and consulting services as appropriate to meet more extensive user needs.

INSTALLATION   Help desk engineers provide telephone assistance
ASSISTANCE   for installation and configuration of personal computer hardware and peripherals, network client software, and application software. Users should have master diskettes and a working knowledge of the personal computer and installation process.

FAULT ISOLATION   Help desk engineers assist in properly identifying and isolating the source of hardware and software problems. In addition, they perform elementary troubleshooting for problems involving a remote host, such as a network server, or host verification and fault isolation on the personal computer client. When problem resolution is expected to be lengthy, the help desk engineer may provide workarounds.

PROBLEM   Help desk engineers assist with the problem resolu-
RESOLUTION   tion or personal computer hardware, software, and netwok problems. If resolution cannot be reached remotely, the engineer refers the problem to the appropriate resource.

PROBLEM   When problem resolution requires additional re-
MANAGEMENT   sources, the help desk engineer transfers the call to the appropriate support resource, such as a local LCM3 support contact, an internal support resource within your organization, or another resource.

BUSINESS HOURS   Assistance is available from Monday through Fri-
COVERAGE   day, excluding LCM3 holidays, from 8: 00 A.M. to 8: 00 P.M. Eastern standard time.

Problem management productivity services includes an on-line help facility to ensure that operator questions are answered.

Optimize Your Investment in Help Desk Hardware

You won't need multiple terminals to access multiple hosts and applications. Problem management productivity services provides support for multiple architectures and lets you move in and out of applications at the touch of a PF key, all from a single workstation. And the proprietary software handles password management, too. Simply specify the applications you want to access automatically from help desk workstations during the installation and customization of problem management productivity services. With problem management productivity services, you can verify the availability and correct operation of applications quickly and easily.

Take advantage of Expert Systems

Problem management productivity services makes each of your help desk operators an expert. Problem management productivity services expert systems will help you determine the source of the problem. Just press a PF key, and a series of questions will prompt the operator to assist in isolating the failure or error. More than twenty-five LCM3 products are included in the expert system knowledge bases—with more being added. And you can develop your own knowledge bases to satisfy your individual requirements.

Problem management productivity services spares you the time-consuming job of looking through pages of product documentation to isolate the source of the problem. With problem management productivity services, there's a simple, time-saving alternative.

Benefit from Electronic Problem Reporting

Once failures and errors have been identified, reporting the problem is easy. That's because product management productivity services links you electronically to LCM3's problem response systems as well as your problem management system (e.g., LCM3's information management system or equivalent).

Your service requests are routed automatically to the apropriate LCM3 service representative for resolution. Your record is queued for entry into your problem management system. This eliminates the redundant task of entering problem-related data more than once.

Speed Up Your Service Response

Problem status updates can be handled quickly and efficiently with problem management productivity services. Your LCM3 service representative, LCM3 dispatch, and your own support functions can electronically update the status of problems through problem management productivity services. One look at your screen and you'll know what action is scheduled, and when.

You'll know when your LCM3 service representative resolves the problem because problem management productivity services will route that information implemented and tested, you can close the problem record from your help desk workstation quickly and easily, with the touch of a single key.

Count on LCM3 for Expert Installation and Support

When you choose management productivity services to help you manage your help desk, an operational support specialist will come to your site to provide the assistance you'll need. First, your operational support specialist helps you assess your current problem management process, and then helps you plan the installation of problem management productivity services. The operational support specialist installs the LCM3 proprietary software and links it to your problem management system. He or she will assist you in customizing problem management productivity services screens so they automatically bring up the information your help desk operators need. LCM3 makes sure all the support functions are connected. And the operational support specialist helps train your staff and demonstrates the ease of building additional knowledge bases.

There's more. You'll receive newsletters with hints, tips, and how-to's that will help you make the most of problem management productivity services. You'll receive on-site support, notification of defects, and answers to your questions, too. And, every year, LCM3 evaluates your problem management process to help you make sure it continues to meet your evolving needs.

Manage and Control the Problem Management Process

Of course, with problem management productivity services, you'll find it much easier to manage and control the problem management process. You'll know how well your help desk is working, because problem management productivity services provides easy access to call statistics through on-line inquiries.

Rely on LCM3 for Improved Productivity

When you choose problem management productivity services, you give your help desk operators a system that's as sophisticated as the ones they support. And you benefit from improved productivity, savings on equipment, and the enhanced effectiveness of your support group. You can reduce the skill needed to staff your help desk while you reduce errors and the need for documentation with the aid of expert systems.

Epilogue

*T*HIS WRAP-UP IS BEING WRITTEN JUST A FEW WEEKS BEFORE *The Virtual Help Desk* becomes a virtual reality, i.e., it hits the street. It's a somewhat frustrating time/event because, since it's so near the end of working on the book, and because we've just proofread the typeset manuscript, we realize that parts of the document are already out of date. There are ideas or issues that are so new, it is impossible to stop and insert them for you, the readers', benefit. The action and change relating to help desk is so rapid *nothing* would get published if we waited for a hiatus in the help desk developments. Things are moving too fast.

The fact that some of the pages herein may be out of date already is actually *good news* for you. It means you are working in one of the most exciting, dynamic and growing segments of the world economy. Besides, most of the ideas in here are still very much alive and valid, notwithstanding their age.

Let us make clear that this is not an apology, by any means. We firmly believe that you will get a number of breakthrough ideas and thoughts from reading this book. All for under $30.00. Some of the best ideas are those triggered by something someone else says. Hopefully this will be the case and some of our thoughts will jog your mind into innovations of your own. If you disagree with us or believe we have perpetrated errors of commission and/or omission, please let us know. And, if for any reason you aren't satisfied with the book, let us know why and we'll see you get a refund, somehow. Remember all our emphasis on customer satisfaction?

Today we listened to a talk at the Wang Center in Boston by Bill Gates, sponsored by the Boston Computer Society, of which he is a loyal member. The messages were all about PC empowerment and the connectivity that makes the world go round and round, and that everyone is so stressed out that we need to use PCs (and of course Microsoft) to "recreate simplicity." Everything is becoming too complex today and we need to let the PC make our jobs and tasks easier. Microsoft really believes this, as there are 40,000 computers available to their 18,000 workers, each of whom does his own scheduling, travel planning, phone answering, and so forth. The administration function within Microsoft has been outsourced to its employees! We also learned at the same meeting that the *Inc*™ (magazine) 500 list of the fastest growing and financially successful private start-up companies were polled last year about using the Internet. Only two percent used the Internet last year, while over fifty percent are using it this year. This microcosm of the Internet landscape reflects the explosive interest in it as a "connectivity" tool and as a potential sales builder. The Microsoft folks presented a case study about a Seattle Nissan™-Volvo™ car dealer, Mr. Rood, who was having problems growing his market. He put his showroom on the Internet and sold over 400 cars, at an average price of $32,000—in less than a year, with little or no human intervention. That, in case you're trying to do the mental math is $14.8 million!!! It's so successful that he has sold his dealership for megabucks and is now peddling the Internet showroom idea.

We heard ideas about help desks and outsourcing them to experts such as Digital Equipment Corporation. One idea mentioned to relieve stress and accommodate an important activity is to set up a help desk over the network for PTA type meetings with your children's teachers. Having an on-line ability to communicate back and forth with parents and teachers would obviate some of the much dreaded plenary sessions at PTA when you're tired and not in the mood to hear the treasurer's report on the last cookie sale.

Yesterday, we visited one of the largest worldwide computer firms to check out their business unit that sells help desks—only help desks. On a day when the Dow Jones Industrial averge reached a record high of over 5000, another record was being posted. This firm's help desk products and services business is going to reach $100 million this year! What's more interesting is the fact that their help desk business is growing at a triple-digit percentage rate.

The help desk or management center is here to stay.

To summarize, we've talked a lot about process. Process that involves the help desk. Let's none of us forget that the process, however, absolutely and unequivocally takes a back seat to the business. Help desks are vital tools in running the business and they can be the focal point of your customers' entry into your enterprise. You, the help desk professional, play a very significant part in representing your company. As the chief liaison, this is very important because your customers' next purchases may actually depend on how you handle this key role. This brings up another key point which we mentioned in the book but will reiterate. It's important. We need to be better ambassadors for our help desk function to internal colleagues, bosses and co-workers. Our important jobs and accomplishments as help desk folks are critical to our companies' successes, and we need to discreetly, but without hesitation, remind our fellow-workers and top management what we do and how we affect the business. The atmosphere and opportunities in the help desk world are humongous and breathtaking. Have a tremendous ride!

Index